THE

POWER

OF

STARTING

Why Beginning Matters More
Than Being Ready

MANUEL ROSENDO

ROSENDO PUBLISHING

Rosendo Publishing
An imprint of Vridge Publishing
Copyright © 2025 by Manuel Rosendo

Requests for permission should be addressed to the publisher at:
Rosendo Publishing
Pembroke Pines, Florida, USA

Disclaimer

This book is intended for informational and inspirational purposes only. The author is not a licensed therapist, financial advisor, attorney, or medical professional. Any actions taken based on the content of this book are done so at the reader's own discretion and risk.

The author makes no guarantees regarding outcomes, results, or success. Individual results will vary based on effort, decisions, and circumstances.

Trademarks

All trademarks, service marks, product names, and logos mentioned in this book are the property of their respective owners and are used for identification purposes only. Their use does not imply endorsement.

ISBN: 978-1-971266-01-5

Library of Congress Control Number: Not assigned

Printed in the United States of America

First Edition

For those who carried responsibility before they carried
dreams— and still found the courage to begin.

To my family.
To Ruth, for believing in me
even when the vision wasn't clear
and the road wasn't easy.

To my children, Kali, Alex, and Liam—
may this book remind you
that courage matters more than certainty
and starting matters more than perfection.

Everything I build is for you.

Contents

Authors Note

I didn't write this book because I figured something out early. I wrote it because I didn't.

For a long time, I lived in the space between knowing and doing. I could see what I wanted clearly enough to feel it pulling at me—but not clearly enough to move without hesitation. I understood ideas. I understood systems. I understood psychology, risk, responsibility, and consequence. What I didn't understand—until much later—was why understanding wasn't enough.

This book was born out of that tension.

I've spent years building companies, rebuilding after failures, carrying responsibility for other people's livelihoods, and doing what needed to be done long before I ever felt free to do what I wanted to do. From the outside, it looked like progress. From the inside, it often felt like postponement. Not because I was lazy or afraid of effort—but because starting something that mattered to me felt heavier than starting things that were expected of me.

At some point, I realized that waiting had become a skill. A sophisticated one. I could justify delay with logic. I could explain hesitation with responsibility. I could dress fear up as wisdom and call it maturity. And for a while, that worked. Until it didn't.

This book is not about motivation.

It's not about chasing your passion.

It's not about quitting your job, burning your life down, or reinventing yourself overnight.

It's about something quieter—and harder.

It's about understanding the forces that keep intelligent, capable, good people from starting the lives they feel called toward. It's about the invisible agreements we make with safety, identity, and approval. It's about how fear learns to speak in reasonable voices. And it's about the small, unglamorous, deeply human act of beginning anyway.

You don't need to read this book quickly.

You don't need to agree with everything in it.

You don't need to turn every page into action.

This is not a manual.

It's a mirror.

Some chapters may feel like they're describing you. Others may feel uncomfortable. That's intentional. Not to judge you—but to reflect something you already know and may not have named yet. Take your time. Let it land where it lands. There is nothing here you need to force.

If there is one thing I hope you don't do, it's this: don't use this book as another place to wait.

Not wait for clarity.

Not wait for confidence.

Not wait for permission.

Let it be a companion, not a hiding place.

If you begin something while reading this—even something small—then the book has already done its job. And if you don't, that's okay too. Awareness is a beginning of its own.

This book exists because I learned, slowly and imperfectly, that starting is not an event reserved for the brave or the free. It's a practice available to anyone willing to stay in relationship with their life.

I hope it helps you do the same.

—Manuel Rosendo

Chapter 1
The Day You Almost Started

There is a moment that comes quietly, so quietly that most people miss it entirely. It does not announce itself as a turning point or arrive with confidence in its voice. It slips into your awareness during ordinary moments—while driving the same route you've driven a thousand times, while lying awake at night replaying conversations that no longer matter, or while scrolling past someone else's life that feels strangely familiar. The thought appears without explanation and without a plan attached to it: *What if I did something else?* It lingers just long enough to make your chest tighten before you push it away. You remind yourself that now isn't the right time, that you have responsibilities, that it would be reckless to disrupt what you've built. You tell yourself you'll think about it later, when things slow down, when you're more prepared. And just like that, the moment passes.

You don't walk away from it because you're afraid of work. You walk away because you've been trained to. Over time, you learned which thoughts were safe to entertain and which ones were better left alone. You learned that dreaming too loudly made people uncomfortable, that wanting more required explanation, and that stability was something to protect at all costs. Somewhere along the way, you absorbed the idea that starting something new was a luxury reserved for people with fewer obligations or more certainty. So instead of starting, you became responsible. You became reliable. You became the kind of person others could count on, even as you quietly stopped counting on yourself.

The conditioning began early, long before you had the language to recognize it. School rewarded compliance more than curiosity, correct answers more than meaningful questions. Progress was linear, predictable, and measured by external approval. You learned that success came from following instructions and avoiding mistakes, and that deviation carried consequences. The message was never explicit, but it was consistent: there is a right path, and your job is to stay on it. Creativity, risk, and self-direction were tolerated only when they fit neatly inside the existing system. Over time, this framework became internalized, shaping not just what you did, but how you evaluated yourself.

As an adult, the rules evolved but never disappeared. They simply took on more sophisticated language. Be realistic. Be practical. Don't throw away what you've worked so hard to build. The cage didn't feel like a cage because it came wrapped in praise and concern. People admired your discipline, your consistency, your ability to "keep it together." You learned to equate discomfort with irresponsibility and desire with danger. Wanting something different began to feel like a betrayal—not just of others' expectations, but of your own identity. After all, if you were the kind of person who took risks, wouldn't you have done it already?

What makes this so disorienting is that your life likely works. You function. You provide. You handle problems when they arise. You may even succeed by conventional standards. But beneath that competence lives a persistent unease, a sense that you are living adjacent to your own potential rather than inside it. It's not dramatic. It doesn't show up as constant misery. It shows up as quiet dissatisfaction, as envy you feel guilty for, as a low-grade restlessness that never quite leaves. You don't hate your life—you just don't feel fully inside it.

There are moments when the gap becomes impossible to ignore. When exhaustion strips away your usual defenses. When you watch someone else take a leap you once imagined for yourself. When a milestone birthday, a loss, or a health scare forces you to confront time in a way you can't rationalize away. In those moments, you feel it clearly: there is a version of you that never got a chance to try. And the grief isn't about failure—it's about abandonment. You didn't lose because you tried and failed. You lost because you never started.

Still, starting feels heavier than staying. The fear isn't just about money, stability, or logistics. It's about identity. If you begin and struggle, you risk discovering that you're not as capable as you hoped. If you begin and fail, you risk rewriting the story you've been telling yourself about who you are. If you begin and succeed, you risk outgrowing the life and relationships that once defined you. Staying where you are allows everything to remain intact. Starting threatens to rearrange it all.

So you prepare instead. Preparation feels safe. Research feels productive. Thinking feels responsible. You refine the idea in your head, adjusting it until it feels smarter, more defensible, more polished. You tell yourself you're waiting for clarity, not avoiding action. But clarity rarely arrives before movement. What arrives instead is fatigue—the kind that comes from carrying an unlived life alongside the one you're already managing.

This is how dreams quietly go to sleep. Not through rejection, but through postponement. Not through failure, but through delay. And postponement is socially acceptable. No one questions "someday." No one challenges "when the time is right." No one calls it fear when it's dressed as patience. But your body knows the difference. It knows when comfort has turned into confinement. It knows when the life you've built no longer fits the person you're becoming.

If any of this feels uncomfortably familiar, it's important to understand this: you are not broken, lazy, or unmotivated. You are conditioned. You were taught—carefully and repeatedly—how to survive, not how to begin. And conditioning, once recognized, can be undone. Not with force, not with bravado, and not with a dramatic leap. But with awareness. Because the moment you see why you haven't started, you loosen the grip of the forces that kept you still.

This book does not begin by asking you to act. It begins by asking you to notice. To see the patterns that shaped you, the fears you learned to normalize, and the rules you never agreed to but still obey. Starting comes later. For now, awareness is enough. Because nothing changes the trajectory of a life faster than the realization that staying has a cost—and that cost has been quietly compounding for years.

Chapter 2
The Invisible Cage

No one ever hands you the cage. There is no ceremony, no warning, no moment where someone looks you in the eye and explains that the life you are about to build will one day feel too small for you. The cage is constructed quietly, patiently, over years, using materials so familiar that they feel harmless—expectations, praise, rules, advice, and love. By the time you are old enough to question it, the structure is already in place, and you have learned how to move comfortably within it. You can stretch your arms. You can rearrange the furniture. You can even decorate the inside. What you cannot easily imagine is stepping outside of it, because you have been taught—slowly and thoroughly—that outside is dangerous.

From the beginning, the message is consistent. Do well in school. Get good grades. Don't fall behind. Follow the path that has already been proven to work. Education is presented not as a tool for exploration, but as insurance against uncertainty. A degree becomes a shield, a job becomes a fortress, and stability becomes the highest virtue. These lessons are rarely malicious. They are passed down by people who wanted you to be safe, who believed that predictability was the same thing as security. But safety, when elevated above all else, quietly rewires how you relate to possibility. You learn not to ask, *What do I want?* but *What is acceptable?*

Over time, the invisible cage stops feeling like an external structure and starts feeling like common sense. You learn to measure decisions by how little disruption they cause. You become fluent in the language of reasonability. Is this realistic? Is this responsible? What will people think? These questions begin to shape not just your choices, but your desires. You start editing yourself before the world ever has to. Dreams that cannot immediately justify themselves are quietly dismissed. Ideas that don't come with guarantees are labeled immature or reckless. Wanting more begins to feel naïve, especially when you already have what others would call a "good life."

This is where the confusion between security and fulfillment takes root. Security answers one question very well: *Will I be okay?* Fulfillment asks a different and far more unsettling one: *Is this who I am meant to be?* Society excels at preparing people to be okay. It is far less comfortable with people who want to be alive. So when a deeper longing emerges—when you feel pulled toward something more meaningful, more expressive, more aligned—it feels suspicious. You tell yourself you should be grateful. You remind yourself of your responsibilities. You downplay the discomfort and assume it's a phase, stress, or restlessness that will pass. But it doesn't pass. It adapts.

The invisible cage does not crush desire; it delays it. It teaches you to postpone what matters under the promise of future permission. *Later, when things calm down. Later, when I'm more established. Later, when it's safer.* You tell yourself you're being patient, not afraid. Responsible, not resistant. Yet years go by, and the version of you who was supposed to emerge "later" remains just out of reach. The cage thrives on delay because delay feels rational. Delay allows you to believe you are still honoring your dream, even as you avoid it.

What makes the cage so powerful is that it is socially enforced. When you stay inside it, you are rewarded. You receive validation, approval, and reassurance. People tell you that you're doing the right thing, that you're smart, that you're lucky to have what you have. When you consider stepping outside of it, the energy shifts. Encouragement turns into concern. Support turns into questioning. *Are you sure? Have you really thought this through? Isn't that risky?* These responses are rarely intended to stop you, but they have that effect nonetheless. They remind you that stepping outside the cage means standing alone, at least for a while.

Eventually, the rules become internal, and this is where the cage becomes hardest to escape. You stop needing external approval because you have learned to withhold it from yourself. You stop listening to your instincts because you have learned to mistrust them. You stop asking what excites you and start asking what makes sense. Even your dreams adapt to the cage. They become smaller, safer, more respectable. You imagine versions of success that fit neatly within what others recognize as legitimate. The bolder visions—the ones that scare you and light you up at the same time—are quietly shelved.

This internal policing creates a strange contradiction. On one hand, you feel free. No one is actively stopping you. On the other hand, you feel trapped by forces you can't quite name. You tell yourself you have choices, but every choice seems to lead back to the same place. The cage doesn't limit your options; it limits your imagination. It defines what feels possible long before action ever enters the picture.

The tragedy is not that the cage exists. Every culture builds one. Order, predictability, and conformity make societies easier to manage. The tragedy is that most people never realize they are inside it. They mistake familiarity for truth and stability for alignment. When discomfort arises—as boredom, anxiety, resentment, or quiet dissatisfaction—they assume something is wrong with them. They work harder, distract themselves more, or numb the feeling with busyness, entertainment, or consumption. Rarely do they question the structure itself.

The invisible cage is not designed to keep you from success. It is designed to keep you predictable. Predictable workers. Predictable consumers. Predictable lives. It favors order over possibility and consistency over growth. And it is remarkably effective because it rarely feels oppressive. It feels reasonable. Sensible. Mature. Escaping it does not require rebellion or recklessness. It requires something far more uncomfortable: awareness. The willingness to see that many of the rules you live by were created to help you belong, not to help you become.

Here is the truth most people never confront: the cage is not outside of you. It lives in the assumptions you rarely question, the fears you justify as practicality, and the voice in your head that tells you to wait until it's safe. As long as the cage remains invisible, it feels impossible to leave. But the moment you begin to see it clearly—not as an enemy, but as a construct—you gain something quietly powerful. Choice. Not the kind of choice that demands immediate action, but the kind that shifts how you see your own life.

Because once you recognize the cage, something else becomes undeniable. The door was never locked. You stayed because you believed you were supposed to. And belief, once examined, loses its grip. You may not be ready to step outside yet. That's okay. Seeing the cage is the first act of freedom. Everything that follows begins there.

Chapter 3
The Psychology of Stuck

Being stuck rarely feels dramatic. It doesn't arrive with panic or despair. Most of the time, it feels like stillness disguised as stability. You wake up, move through your day, handle what needs to be handled, and repeat the process tomorrow. On the surface, everything appears functional. But underneath that rhythm lives a quiet tension—a sense that something inside you wants to move while the rest of your life insists on staying put. You don't feel trapped in a way you can point to. You feel trapped in a way that's hard to explain without sounding ungrateful.

What makes this state so confusing is that stuckness doesn't feel like failure. It feels like waiting. Waiting for clarity. Waiting for confidence. Waiting for the right moment, the right conditions, the right version of yourself to show up. You tell yourself you're being patient, strategic, thoughtful. And in many ways, you are. But patience becomes a problem when it turns into paralysis, and strategy becomes avoidance when it never leads to movement. The psychology of stuck is not about laziness or lack of ambition. It's about how the mind protects identity.-

At the center of this protection is fear—but not the kind people usually talk about. Most people assume fear of failure is what keeps them from starting, but failure is only part of the equation. Fear of judgment runs just as deep. What will people think if you try and fall short? What will they say if you change direction, pivot, or outgrow the role they're used to seeing you in? Humans are wired for belonging, and belonging is often threatened when you step outside the expected path. The mind understands this intuitively. It calculates the social cost of change long before you consciously acknowledge it.

Then there is a quieter fear, one that is rarely named: fear of success. Success changes things. It alters relationships, routines, and expectations. It forces you to become someone new, and becoming someone new often means leaving parts of your old life behind. The mind resists this not because success is bad, but because it is destabilizing. Staying where you are allows your identity to remain intact. You know who you are here. You know how to perform this version of yourself. Starting something new threatens that familiarity.

This is where identity paralysis takes hold. At some level, you ask yourself a question you may not even realize you're asking: *If I start and it doesn't work, who am I then?* But there's an equally unsettling version on the other side: *If I start and it does work, who will I have to become?* Both outcomes challenge the story you've been telling yourself about your life. And the mind, designed to preserve coherence and predictability, often decides that not starting is the safest option.

Clarity, which people so often claim they're waiting for, is another misunderstood barrier. The truth is that clarity is frequently avoided, not lacking. Clarity demands commitment. Once you see what you truly want, you can no longer hide behind uncertainty. You can no longer pretend you don't know. Staying unclear gives you room to delay, to hedge, to keep options open without choosing any of them. The mind prefers ambiguity when clarity would force action.

Familiarity plays its role here as well. The known, even when it's uncomfortable, feels safer than the unknown. You understand your current frustrations. You know how to manage them. You've built coping mechanisms, routines, and explanations around them. The unknown, on the other hand, has no script. It offers possibility, but it also offers unpredictability. The brain, wired to minimize risk, often chooses familiar discomfort over unfamiliar opportunity. This is why people stay in unfulfilling jobs, stagnant relationships, and lives that no longer fit. Not because they don't want more, but because more comes wrapped in uncertainty.

Psychologically, this state is reinforced through subtle patterns that compound over time. Each time you hesitate, the mind records it as evidence. *See? This is dangerous. Better not try.* Each time you postpone, the behavior becomes normalized. Over time, inaction becomes part of your identity. You stop seeing yourself as someone who starts things and begin seeing yourself as someone who thinks about starting things. This shift is quiet but powerful. Identity follows behavior, even when that behavior is doing nothing.

Another layer of stuckness comes from cognitive dissonance—the discomfort that arises when your actions don't align with your beliefs. You believe you are capable, intelligent, and driven, yet your life does not reflect the dreams you carry. To reduce the discomfort, the mind adjusts the narrative. You tell yourself you don't really want it that badly. You convince yourself it's not the right time. You downplay the importance of the dream altogether. This self-justification protects your self-image, but it also keeps you trapped.

Learned helplessness can quietly settle in as well, especially if past attempts didn't go as planned. When effort doesn't produce the expected result, the mind learns a dangerous lesson: *Trying doesn't matter.* Over time, this belief can generalize, leading you to disengage even when circumstances change. You stop trusting your ability to influence outcomes, and waiting becomes your default mode.

What's important to understand is that none of this is a personal flaw. These patterns exist because the human brain evolved to keep you alive, not to help you fulfill your potential. It prioritizes certainty over meaning, safety over growth, and belonging over self-expression. When you feel stuck, your brain is doing exactly what it was designed to do. The problem is that survival strategies make poor life strategies.

The psychology of stuck thrives on one central illusion: that movement requires confidence. In reality, confidence is a byproduct of movement, not a prerequisite for it. The mind insists you feel ready before you begin, but readiness is something that emerges through action. Waiting for it is like waiting for strength before lifting the weight. The longer you wait, the heavier it feels.

Understanding this doesn't immediately free you. Awareness alone doesn't dissolve years of conditioning. But it does something crucial. It reframes your experience. You stop seeing stuckness as a personal failure and start recognizing it as a predictable psychological state. And what is predictable can be interrupted.

This chapter is not meant to push you into action. It's meant to help you see the forces at play when you don't act. To recognize that the hesitation you feel is not a verdict on your ability, but a signal from a mind that is trying to protect you using outdated rules. The moment you understand that, something shifts. You stop fighting yourself. You stop shaming yourself. And in that space—between understanding and movement—the possibility of starting quietly begins to form.

Chapter 4
Pain & Pleasure Wiring: The Brain's Betrayal

Your brain is not designed to help you build your dream life. That statement alone makes many people uncomfortable, because we like to believe that if we just think clearly enough, want something badly enough, or discipline ourselves hard enough, our mind will eventually get on board. The truth is far less flattering and far more liberating: your brain's primary job is not fulfillment, growth, or meaning—it is survival. And survival, from the brain's perspective, means avoiding pain, minimizing risk, and conserving energy. Everything else is secondary.

This wiring made perfect sense when survival depended on avoiding predators and conserving calories. It makes far less sense in a modern world where the greatest threats are not physical danger, but regret, stagnation, and unlived potential. Yet the brain has not caught up. It still treats uncertainty as a threat, discomfort as danger, and unfamiliar paths as something to be avoided. When you think about starting something new—a business, a creative pursuit, a relationship, a new version of yourself—your brain doesn't see opportunity. It sees risk.

This is where the pain–pleasure principle quietly sabotages you. The brain is constantly running a calculation in the background: *Will this bring me pain, or will this bring me pleasure?* But here's the catch—it is biased toward short-term outcomes. Immediate discomfort is weighted far more heavily than long-term reward. Starting something new promises meaning, growth, and fulfillment, but it also guarantees uncertainty, effort, and the possibility of embarrassment or failure. To the brain, that immediate discomfort feels far more real than a future payoff it cannot yet experience.

So, the brain intervenes. Not with alarms or panic, but with rational-sounding thoughts. *Now isn't the right time. You should think this through more. You're already tired. Why add stress?* These thoughts feel reasonable because they are rooted in the brain's mandate to keep you safe and comfortable. What you experience as procrastination or lack of motivation is often your nervous system choosing familiarity over possibility.

This wiring explains why so many people replace starting with numbing. When action feels threatening, the brain seeks alternative sources of pleasure—ones that are immediate, predictable, and low-risk. Scrolling. Streaming. Snacking. Shopping. Staying busy with tasks that feel productive but require no vulnerability. These behaviors are not signs of weakness. They are coping mechanisms. They deliver small doses of dopamine without requiring you to step into uncertainty. They help you feel temporarily relieved without changing anything that matters.

Busyness deserves special attention here, because it is one of the most socially acceptable forms of avoidance. When you are busy, no one questions your lack of movement. In fact, they often praise it. You can fill your days with obligations, responsibilities, and low-stakes tasks and still never take a single step toward the life you want. The brain loves busyness because it creates the illusion of progress without triggering the fear response associated with starting. You feel occupied, even important, while staying safely inside the known.

Over time, this pattern strengthens. Each time you avoid discomfort and choose short-term relief, the brain learns. *This works. This keeps us safe.* The neural pathways associated with avoidance become easier to activate, while the pathways associated with courageous action weaken from disuse. This is not a moral failing. It is neuroplasticity in action. The brain adapts to what you repeatedly do. And if what you repeatedly do is avoid starting, avoidance becomes your default.

This is why people often say they feel "addicted" to distraction or comfort. It's not addiction in the traditional sense—it's conditioning. The brain has learned that scrolling feels better than risking rejection, that staying busy feels better than facing uncertainty, that comfort feels better than courage in the short term. The problem is that short-term pleasure comes with a long-term cost. It postpones fulfillment. It dulls desire. It turns restlessness into resignation.

There is another betrayal hidden in this wiring: the brain's resistance to uncertainty. Even when certainty equals misery, the brain often prefers it over the unknown. A job you dislike, a relationship that has grown stale, a life that feels smaller than you know it could be—all of these are predictable. You know how to survive them. The unknown, on the other hand, has no guarantees. It could bring joy, freedom, and alignment, but it could also bring struggle. To the brain, struggle is unacceptable unless it is familiar.

This explains a painful paradox: people will tolerate years of quiet dissatisfaction to avoid weeks or months of uncertainty. They will choose known unhappiness over possible fulfillment because the brain values predictability more than possibility. And when you judge yourself for this choice, you miss the deeper truth—you are not choosing misery; your brain is choosing certainty.

Chapter 5
Cultural Myths That Keep People Small

Most of the beliefs that shape your life do not feel like beliefs at all. They feel like facts. They feel like common sense, wisdom passed down through experience, lessons learned the hard way. You don't remember choosing them, and you certainly don't remember questioning them. They simply became part of the mental landscape you navigate every day. This is how cultural myths work. They don't announce themselves as limitations; they present themselves as protection. And because they are repeated so often—by family, institutions, media, and even people you admire—they begin to feel unquestionable.

One of the most powerful of these myths is the idea that you need to be ready before you begin. Readiness is portrayed as a prerequisite for action, something you earn through preparation, confidence, or experience. On the surface, this sounds reasonable. Who wouldn't want to feel prepared before stepping into something new? But readiness is a moving target. There is always more to learn, more to plan, more to perfect. Waiting to feel ready becomes an endless loop that rewards hesitation and punishes momentum. The myth of readiness keeps people stalled not because they lack ability, but because they believe they must eliminate uncertainty before moving forward.

Closely tied to this is the myth that you need more—more money, more time, more confidence, more credentials—before you can start. This belief is especially seductive because it feels practical. It gives you something to chase that isn't the thing itself. You tell yourself that once you have enough saved, enough knowledge, or enough clarity, then you'll begin. What goes unexamined is that "enough" is rarely defined. It shifts as soon as you get close. The goalposts move, and starting remains just out of reach. This myth allows you to feel responsible while staying safely within the familiar.

Another deeply ingrained belief is that others have it figured out. You look at people who have started businesses, changed careers, built meaningful relationships, or followed unconventional paths, and you assume they possessed something you don't—confidence, certainty, courage. You imagine they knew what they were doing from the beginning. This comparison is rarely fair or accurate. You see their results, not their confusion. You see their highlight reel, not their early missteps. But the myth persists, and it reinforces the idea that you are somehow behind, late, or unqualified.

The myth of "it's too late" may be the most devastating of all. Time becomes a weapon turned inward. You tell yourself you should have started earlier, that the window has closed, that the cost of beginning now is too high. Age, responsibilities, and past choices are used as evidence against you. What this belief ignores is that time will pass regardless. The only difference between starting now and not starting is what exists on the other side of that passing time. The myth of lateness keeps people frozen in regret rather than moving toward possibility.

These myths persist because they are reinforced at every level of society. Institutions favor predictability. Systems reward compliance. Media celebrates outcomes while skipping over the messy beginnings that made them possible. Even well-meaning advice often carries the same underlying message: don't move until it's safe. Don't disrupt what works. Don't risk being wrong. The cultural narrative prizes stability and certainty, even when those things come at the cost of meaning and growth.

What makes these myths particularly powerful is that they are self-reinforcing. When you don't start, the myth feels validated. *See? You weren't ready. See? You needed more time.* Each delay strengthens the belief that waiting was the right choice. Over time, these myths stop feeling external and start feeling like your own thoughts. You no longer hear them as societal programming; you hear them as your inner voice.

This internalization creates a subtle form of control. You become your own gatekeeper, your own skeptic, your own critic. You dismiss your desires before they can fully form. You rationalize your inaction with language that sounds mature and responsible. You tell yourself you're being cautious, not afraid. Realistic, not resistant. But beneath that logic lives a quieter truth: these myths keep you small because they keep you waiting.

It's important to understand that these beliefs are not accidents. A culture that runs on predictability and consumption benefits when people stay within predefined roles. Big dreams challenge systems. Questioning norms introduces uncertainty. Starting something new requires energy, attention, and courage—resources that are easier to manage when they are directed elsewhere. This doesn't mean there is a conspiracy against you, but it does mean that the default narrative is not designed to help you break free.

The danger of these myths is not that they are obviously false. It's that they are partially true. Preparation matters. Resources help. Timing influences outcomes. But when these truths are taken to extremes, they become excuses that masquerade as wisdom. They keep you thinking when what you need is movement. They keep you analyzing when what you need is experience. They keep you safe when what you need is growth.

This chapter is not asking you to reject every piece of advice you've ever received or to act recklessly in defiance of reason. It's asking you to notice which beliefs quietly limit your choices. To question whether the rules you live by were meant to guide you—or to contain you. Myths lose their power when they are named. Once you see them for what they are—stories repeated until they feel like truth—you gain the ability to choose differently.

You may not be ready to dismantle these beliefs yet. That's okay. Awareness comes before change. But the next time you hear the familiar refrain—*not yet, not now, not enough*—you'll recognize it for what it is. Not a fact. Not a verdict. Just a story. And stories, once questioned, no longer get to decide the shape of your life.

Chapter 6
The Frameworks Beneath the Surface

By the time most people begin questioning why they feel stuck, they are already exhausted. They've tried motivation. They've read books. They've listened to podcasts, taken notes, and promised themselves that this time would be different. When nothing changes, the conclusion feels personal: *Maybe this is just who I am.* What rarely occurs to them is that their experience is not unique or mysterious. It is patterned. Predictable. Explained—quietly and thoroughly—by psychological frameworks that describe human behavior with unsettling accuracy. These frameworks are not labels meant to trap you; they are maps meant to orient you. And once you see the map, you stop blaming yourself for getting lost.

One of the most influential forces at work is **status quo bias**—the brain's tendency to prefer things to stay the same, even when change would objectively improve your situation.

This bias operates beneath conscious thought. It doesn't ask whether your current life is fulfilling; it simply assumes that what exists is safer than what doesn't. The familiar becomes automatically preferable, not because it is better, but because it is known. When you consider starting something new, the mind subtly exaggerates the risks and minimizes the potential rewards. Staying put feels neutral, even when it slowly drains you. Movement feels dangerous, even when it might set you free.

Closely tied to this is **loss aversion**, the tendency to feel potential losses more intensely than equivalent gains. Psychologically, losing something hurts roughly twice as much as gaining something feels good. This imbalance has profound consequences. When you contemplate starting, your mind fixates on what you might lose—time, money, reputation, stability—rather than what you might gain. The dream remains abstract, distant, and uncertain, while the losses feel immediate and tangible. This is why people cling to situations they have outgrown. The pain of leaving feels sharper than the promise of what could replace it.

Another framework quietly shaping your behavior is **learned helplessness**. When repeated effort fails to produce meaningful change, the mind learns a dangerous lesson: effort doesn't matter. Over time, this belief generalizes. You stop trying not because you don't care, but because trying has felt futile in the past. This often happens subtly. A failed business attempt. A relationship that didn't work. A risk that didn't pay off. Instead of interpreting these experiences as part of growth, the mind stores them as evidence against action itself. Eventually, waiting feels wiser than trying.

Then there is **imposter syndrome**, often misunderstood as a lack of confidence when it is actually a conflict of identity. You feel like a fraud not because you are incapable, but because the version of yourself who wants more has not yet been validated by action. You compare your internal uncertainty with other people's external confidence and assume you don't belong. What imposter syndrome really reveals is that you are standing at the edge of expansion. You are attempting to occupy a space your identity hasn't yet caught up to. The discomfort is not a warning sign—it is a transition signal.

Cognitive dissonance adds another layer of complexity. This is the psychological tension that arises when your beliefs and actions don't align. You believe you are capable, thoughtful, and driven, yet your life does not reflect the dreams you carry. To relieve the tension, the mind adjusts the story. You downplay the importance of the dream. You convince yourself it was unrealistic anyway. You tell yourself you're happy enough. These justifications protect your self-image, but they also reinforce inaction. The longer this dissonance persists, the more invested you become in defending the life you're already living.

Fear conditioning operates quietly in the background as well. When discomfort or failure is associated with emotional pain—shame, embarrassment, rejection—the brain learns to avoid similar situations in the future. This conditioning doesn't require trauma; it only requires repetition. Each uncomfortable experience strengthens the association. Over time, the mere thought of starting triggers a stress response. Your body reacts before your mind can reason with it. What you experience as anxiety is often your nervous system recalling past discomfort and trying to prevent it from happening again.

Perhaps the most deeply rooted framework of all is **identity-based resistance to change**. Your identity is built from stories—about who you are, what you're good at, what you're allowed to want, and what you're capable of handling. Starting something new threatens those stories. It asks you to become a beginner again, to risk looking foolish, to step into a role you don't yet know how to perform. The mind resists not because change is bad, but because it destabilizes the narrative that has kept you coherent and socially anchored. Remaining stuck allows your identity to stay intact, even if it no longer fits.

What these frameworks reveal is a humbling truth: staying stuck is not a lack of intelligence or willpower. It is the result of multiple psychological forces pulling in the same direction.

Each one reinforces the others. Status quo bias makes staying feel safe. Loss aversion makes leaving feel costly. Learned helplessness discourages effort. Imposter syndrome questions belonging. Cognitive dissonance rewrites the narrative. Fear conditioning triggers avoidance. Identity resistance locks it all in place. Together, they form a system that favors stillness over motion.

Seeing this system clearly changes the conversation you have with yourself. Instead of asking why you can't just push through, you begin to understand why pushing rarely works. Willpower is no match for a mind that believes it is protecting you. Motivation fades when it is asked to fight identity, fear, and conditioning all at once. This is why most attempts at change fail—not because the desire wasn't real, but because the approach misunderstood the problem.

This chapter is not meant to overwhelm you with theory. It's meant to offer relief. Relief in knowing that your hesitation is not random or personal. Relief in understanding that what feels like a flaw is actually a pattern. And patterns, once recognized, can be interrupted. Not by force, but by awareness and design. When you know the frameworks at work, you stop internalizing the resistance. You stop treating fear as a verdict. You begin to see stuckness as a signal—not that you should stop, but that something inside you is being challenged to evolve.

The frameworks do not disappear overnight. They don't dissolve just because you understand them. But understanding creates distance. And distance creates choice. You are no longer reacting blindly; you are responding consciously. That shift—quiet, internal, and almost imperceptible—is the beginning of change. Before action. Before courage. Before starting. Because nothing moves until you stop mistaking the system for yourself.

The Science Behind What's Really Happening

The ideas explored in this chapter are not philosophical guesses or motivational theory—they are grounded in well-established research from neuroscience, psychology, and behavioral science.

Modern neuroscience shows that the brain is wired primarily for survival, not growth. Research on the amygdala and threat detection demonstrates how uncertainty activates protective responses long before conscious reasoning takes place (LeDoux, 1996). This explains why insight alone rarely leads to action—because resistance is often emotional before it is logical.

Studies in behavioral psychology confirm that identity follows behavior, not the other way around. Research by Dr. James Clear and earlier work on habit formation show that repeated small actions reshape self-perception over time, reinforcing new identities through evidence rather than intention (Lally et al., 2010).

Additionally, work in Self-Determination Theory (Deci & Ryan, 2000) shows that sustainable motivation emerges when actions align with autonomy, competence, and internal meaning—rather than pressure, discipline, or external validation. This is why forcing change through willpower alone so often leads to burnout.

Finally, studies on cognitive load and decision fatigue demonstrate how overthinking and excessive planning can actually reduce the likelihood of action (Baumeister et al., 1998). When the mind is overwhelmed, the brain defaults to familiarity, not progress.

I don't share this from theory alone—I share it from lived experience. I was once caught inside these same psychological frameworks, mistaking them for truth instead of recognizing them as patterns at work. As I began to understand what was really happening beneath the surface, I didn't eliminate them—I learned to create distance. The noise didn't disappear, but its volume lowered enough that it no longer ran the show.

_____

Key References

- LeDoux, J. (1996). *The Emotional Brain*. Simon & Schuster.

- Deci, E. L., & Ryan, R. M. (2000). Intrinsic and Extrinsic Motivations: Classic Definitions and New Directions. *Contemporary Educational Psychology.*
- Lally, P., van Jaarsveld, C. H. M., Potts, H. W. W., & Wardle, J. (2010). How Are Habits Formed? *European Journal of Social Psychology.*
- Baumeister, R. F., et al. (1998). Ego Depletion: Is the Active Self a Limited Resource? *Journal of Personality and Social Psychology.*

Chapter 7

The Lie of the Big Leap

Most people believe that change happens in a moment. A decisive break. A bold announcement. A dramatic exit from the life that no longer fits. This belief is everywhere—embedded in stories of overnight success, viral transformations, and carefully edited narratives that skip straight from dissatisfaction to triumph. It's an appealing idea. Clean. Cinematic. And deeply misleading. The lie of the big leap convinces people that starting requires a singular act of bravery, when in reality, that belief is one of the greatest barriers to beginning at all.

The fantasy usually looks something like this: one day you'll wake up with clarity, confidence, and courage all aligned. You'll know exactly what to do, feel ready to do it, and have the emotional energy to handle whatever comes next. In that imagined moment, fear will be quiet, doubt will be absent, and the risk will somehow feel justified. Until then, you wait. You tell yourself that starting now—without certainty—would be irresponsible. The big leap becomes a psychological requirement, and because it feels impossible, inaction becomes inevitable.

What this myth ignores is how human beings actually change. Transformation rarely happens through rupture. It happens through accumulation. Small decisions made repeatedly. Quiet shifts in behavior that don't look impressive from the outside but radically alter your internal trajectory. The big leap myth fails because it demands too much of a nervous system that is already wired to avoid risk. It frames starting as an all-or-nothing event, which triggers fear long before action can occur.

This is why starting feels overwhelming. You're not afraid of the first step—you're afraid of everything you believe the first step commits you to. When you imagine beginning, your mind doesn't stop at today's action. It races ahead to consequences you haven't earned yet. What if this fails? What if it works? What will people think? What will I have to give up? The leap grows larger and more threatening in your imagination until it feels reckless to even consider it.

In truth, starting is rarely dramatic. It's awkward. It's quiet. It often happens without witnesses. Most beginnings don't feel heroic; they feel lonely and uncertain. They involve doing something before you feel qualified, confident, or supported. They require tolerating the discomfort of being new, visible, and imperfect. The big leap myth erases this reality and replaces it with a standard no real beginning can meet.

Another reason the myth persists is that it allows you to postpone responsibility. If change requires a big leap, then waiting makes sense. You can tell yourself you're not afraid—you're just not ready for something that significant. The problem is that readiness never arrives in the form you're waiting for. Courage is not a prerequisite; it is a response to action. Confidence is not something you summon; it is something you earn through experience. Momentum does not precede movement; it follows it.

The belief in the big leap also distorts how you measure progress. If you expect transformation to feel dramatic, subtle shifts feel insignificant. Small actions are dismissed as meaningless because they don't match the intensity of the imagined breakthrough. You underestimate the power of consistency and overestimate the value of intensity. This leads to cycles of overthinking and underacting—periods of mental preparation followed by continued stagnation.

What rarely gets acknowledged is how deeply lonely the beginning can feel. The big leap myth suggests applause, validation, and support will accompany change. In reality, early movement often happens in silence. No one is watching yet. No one understands what you're doing. The lack of external reinforcement can make you question whether the effort matters at all. This is where many people stop—not because they failed, but because they misinterpreted quiet progress as no progress.

The truth is uncomfortable but freeing: no one is coming to declare the moment safe. There will be no universal signal that you are allowed to begin. The leap you're waiting for is a mirage. What exists instead is a threshold—small, unremarkable, and easily overlooked. Crossing it does not change everything at once. It changes something just enough to make the next step possible.

Starting, in its real form, does not ask you to burn your life down. It asks you to interrupt a pattern. To do something today that the old version of you would postpone. It might be a conversation you've been avoiding, a first draft you don't plan to share, a single outreach, a small experiment that carries no guarantee. These actions feel too minor to matter, which is precisely why they work. They bypass the brain's alarm system. They don't demand a leap—only a shift.

This is the part of the journey that rarely makes it into stories. The part where progress feels slow and fragile. Where doubt hasn't disappeared, but you move anyway. Where the identity you're becoming hasn't fully formed, and the identity you've been living in hasn't quite let go. It's uncomfortable, unglamorous, and deeply human. And it's where real change happens.

The lie of the big leap keeps people waiting for a moment that never comes. The truth is quieter: movement creates permission. Action generates clarity. Each small start provides evidence that the fear was survivable, the uncertainty manageable, and the effort worthwhile. Over time, these small starts compound into something that finally looks like a leap—but by then, it no longer feels like one.

This chapter is not asking you to abandon caution or leap blindly into the unknown. It's asking you to question the belief that starting must feel dramatic to be valid. Most life-changing journeys begin without fireworks. They begin with a decision so small it barely feels like a decision at all. And that is exactly why so many people miss it.

The big leap is not where change begins. It's where stories end. Real beginnings happen earlier, quieter, and closer than you think.

Chapter 8

The One Principle That Changes Everything

If you strip away all the theories, all the frameworks, all the stories we tell ourselves about fear, readiness, and timing, what remains is something almost offensively simple. So simple, in fact, that most people overlook it. They assume anything capable of changing a life must be complex, dramatic, or profound. But the truth rarely works that way. The most powerful shifts are often built on principles so basic they feel incomplete—until you live them.

You've already seen this pattern at work in earlier chapters, even if we didn't name it outright. Each time action created understanding instead of waiting for it, the same truth was quietly operating beneath the surface.

The principle is this: **starting precedes clarity**—not the other way around.

What changes here is not the idea itself, but the recognition of it. Once you see this principle clearly and begin to trust it, it stops being an observation and becomes a turning point—because it explains why so many people remain stuck, and why movement is the one thing that changes everything.

This is the point where many people quietly resist. They nod, but something inside them tightens. Because if clarity does not come first, then the waiting has never been justified. If action creates clarity, then hesitation has not been wisdom—it has been avoidance dressed in logic. This realization can feel unsettling, even confrontational, because it removes the final excuse that has protected you from movement.

From childhood, you were taught that understanding comes before action. Learn first, then do. Prepare thoroughly, then begin. Make sure you know what you're doing before you try. In many areas of life, this makes sense. But when it comes to building a dream, changing direction, or becoming someone new, this order collapses. You cannot think your way into a new identity. You must act your way into it.

Clarity is not something you discover in isolation. It is something you generate through contact with reality. You learn what you want by trying. You learn what you're capable of by moving. You learn what fits by experiencing what doesn't. Every meaningful insight you admire in others was earned through action that came before certainty. They didn't know—they started, and knowing followed.

The mind resists this because it feels backwards. It wants guarantees before effort, confidence before exposure, permission before risk. But life does not offer guarantees in advance. It offers feedback in response to movement. The only way to access that feedback is to begin. Without action, you are trapped in speculation—imagining outcomes, rehearsing fears, and debating possibilities that have never been tested.

This is where the second part of the principle comes into focus: **action creates belief**.

Belief is not a prerequisite for action; it is a consequence of it. You don't believe you can do something and then act—you act, survive the experience, and belief forms afterward. Every time you take a step and nothing catastrophic happens, your nervous system recalibrates. Each action provides evidence. Each piece of evidence weakens the old story and strengthens a new one. Slowly, quietly, belief begins to shift—not because you convinced yourself, but because you proved something to yourself.

This is how confidence is actually built. Not through affirmations or visualization, but through repetition. Doing the thing again and again until the brain updates its model of what is possible. Confidence is memory. It is the accumulation of survived experiences. And the only way to create those memories is to act before you feel ready.

The final piece of the principle is the most transformative and the least discussed: **identity follows behavior.**

You do not become someone new by deciding to be them. You become them by behaving like them long enough that the identity sticks. This is why thinking about change rarely works. Thinking does not challenge identity; action does. When you take a step that contradicts your old self-image, even a small one, it creates friction. That friction forces the mind to adjust. Either the behavior stops, or the identity updates. And when the behavior is repeated, the identity has no choice but to evolve.

This is why starting small is not a compromise—it is a strategy. Small actions are less threatening to the nervous system, but they are still powerful enough to disrupt old patterns. They bypass the brain's resistance while still producing real change. A single conversation. A single attempt. A single decision to move instead of wait. These moments rarely feel life-changing at the time, but they are. They are votes cast for a different future self.

What most people never realize is that every meaningful life change begins the same way. Not with certainty. Not with courage. Not with confidence. But with someone starting before they were ready. Every story of transformation, when traced back far enough, leads to an unremarkable beginning that felt insignificant, risky, or unnecessary at the time. The difference between those who change and those who don't is not talent or luck—it is the willingness to act without guarantees.

This principle does not promise ease. Starting will still feel uncomfortable. Doubt will still show up. Fear will still whisper. The difference is that you stop waiting for those feelings to disappear before you move. You understand that they are not obstacles; they are companions on the path of change. Their presence does not mean you are doing something wrong. It means you are doing something new.

This chapter is not about motivation. Motivation fades. This is about orientation—about flipping the order in which you've been taught to live. You stop asking, *Am I ready?* and start asking, *What is the smallest honest step I can take from where I am?* You stop negotiating with fear and start collecting evidence. You stop trying to become someone new in theory and start practicing it in reality.

Nothing about this principle is flashy. It will not impress people who are committed to staying comfortable. But it works. Quietly. Relentlessly. Over time, it dismantles everything that once kept you stuck. Because once you start—even imperfectly—you are no longer the person who only thinks about starting. And that shift, more than any leap or breakthrough, is what changes the direction of a life.

Starting does not solve everything or guarantee outcomes. But it solves the only problem that matters at the beginning. It breaks the spell of waiting. And once that spell is broken, the journey—your journey—finally has somewhere to go.

Chapter 9
Why Starting Feels So Uncomfortable

If starting is so powerful—if it truly precedes clarity, creates belief, and reshapes identity—then a reasonable question follows: *Why does it feel so bad?* Why does something so necessary feel so unnatural, so heavy, so emotionally charged? Most people assume the discomfort means something is wrong. That the resistance is a sign they are making a mistake. In reality, the discomfort is not a warning—it is a confirmation. It is evidence that something real is happening beneath the surface.

Starting feels uncomfortable because it places you in a psychological no-man's-land. You are no longer fully protected by the old identity, but the new one has not yet taken shape. You have stepped out of certainty without yet arriving at confidence. This in-between space is where the mind struggles most. It prefers clear categories—success or failure, right or wrong, safe or dangerous. Starting lives in none of these. It exists in ambiguity, and ambiguity is deeply unsettling to a nervous system wired for prediction.

The discomfort often shows up first in the body. A tight chest. A shallow breath. Restlessness. Fatigue that feels disproportionate to the effort required. These sensations are easy to misinterpret as signs of incapacity or misalignment. But they are not messages about your ability—they are signals from a nervous system encountering novelty. Your body is adjusting to unfamiliar terrain, recalibrating expectations, and scanning for threat. This is not fear in the dramatic sense; it is uncertainty being processed at a biological level.

Emotionally, starting disrupts the equilibrium you've worked hard to maintain. Even if your current life feels constrained, it is familiar. You know how to operate within it. You know which parts of yourself to show and which to hide. Beginning something new introduces emotional exposure. You are no longer protected by routine or reputation. You risk being seen as inexperienced, uncertain, or imperfect. This vulnerability is uncomfortable not because it is dangerous, but because it is honest.

Another source of discomfort is the loss of fantasy. Before you start, your dream can remain ideal. Untested. Perfect. It exists in a protected mental space where it cannot be criticized or fail. Starting brings the dream into contact with reality, and reality is messy. Ideas don't land perfectly. Effort doesn't always translate into progress. This collision between expectation and experience can feel discouraging, even painful. Many people retreat at this stage, not because the dream was wrong, but because the fantasy was safer than the truth.

There is also a quieter discomfort that few people talk about: the grief of letting go of who you were. Even if that version of you felt limited or unfulfilled, it was known. It carried stories, relationships, and a sense of belonging. Starting something new often requires releasing parts of that identity. You may outgrow roles that once defined you. You may no longer relate to conversations that once felt comfortable. This loss is rarely acknowledged, but it is real. Growth always carries grief alongside it.

The mind often responds to this discomfort by looking for an exit. It offers rationalizations. *This isn't the right time. Maybe this wasn't the right idea. I should stop before I waste more energy.* These thoughts feel protective because they promise relief. If you stop, the discomfort fades. The nervous system settles. The old equilibrium returns. This is why so many people interpret relief as evidence they made the right choice, when in fact it is simply evidence that the threat has been removed.

What makes starting uniquely uncomfortable is that it exposes the gap between intention and reality. You are no longer who you were, but you are not yet who you are becoming. This gap is humbling. It reveals limitations you could previously ignore. It forces you to confront learning curves, mistakes, and uncertainty in real time. For people accustomed to competence and control, this can feel especially destabilizing. It challenges the self-image you've carefully constructed.

And yet, this discomfort serves a purpose. It is the sensation of growth. Just as muscles ache when they are challenged in new ways, the psyche resists when it is stretched beyond familiar boundaries. The discomfort is not telling you to stop; it is telling you that you are doing something you have not done before. It is the feeling of capacity expanding, even if it doesn't feel like progress yet.

The mistake most people make is assuming that comfort is the goal. Comfort feels good, but it is not neutral. Prolonged comfort often signals stagnation. Growth rarely feels soothing at the beginning. It feels awkward, uncertain, and destabilizing. The people who build meaningful lives are not those who avoid discomfort, but those who learn how to stay present within it without retreating.

This chapter is not meant to romanticize struggle or suggest that pain is required for growth. It is meant to normalize discomfort so you stop misreading it. When starting feels uncomfortable, it does not mean you are failing. It means you are transitioning. The unease you feel is not a sign to go back— it is a sign that you have left the old boundary behind.

Understanding this changes your relationship with resistance. Instead of asking, *How do I make this feeling go away?* you begin asking, *What is this feeling trying to teach me?* You stop chasing comfort and start building capacity. You recognize that the early stages of starting are not meant to feel good; they are meant to feel different.

Discomfort does not mean danger. It means unfamiliarity. And unfamiliarity is the price of becoming someone you have never been before. If starting feels uncomfortable, it is not because you are doing it wrong. It is because you are finally doing it at all.

Chapter 10
The Cost of Not Starting

Not starting feels neutral. That is its most dangerous quality. There is no immediate consequence, no dramatic fallout, no obvious loss you can point to and say, *That's what it cost me.* Life continues. Bills get paid. Responsibilities are handled. Days pass. From the outside, nothing appears to be wrong. But neutrality is an illusion. Not starting is never free— it simply charges you slowly, quietly, over time.

The cost begins as something subtle. A low-grade dissatisfaction that you learn to live with. A feeling you dismiss as stress, fatigue, or restlessness. You tell yourself it's normal, that everyone feels this way, that this is just part of adulthood. And maybe it is common—but common does not mean harmless. Over time, that dissatisfaction becomes background noise, something you barely notice until it flares up in moments of silence. Late at night. On long drives. During milestones that are supposed to feel fulfilling but don't quite land the way you expected.

One of the first things not starting costs you is **self-trust**. Each time you feel the pull toward something meaningful and ignore it, you send yourself a message. Not consciously, but internally, at the level where identity is formed. The message is simple: *I don't act on what matters to me.* Over time, that message compounds. You stop taking your own desires seriously. You hesitate before committing to anything that requires courage. Eventually, you don't just doubt your ability to start—you doubt your right to want more in the first place.

Another cost is **emotional energy**. Carrying an unlived life is exhausting. Even when you're not actively thinking about it, the tension is there. It shows up as irritability, apathy, or a sense of being perpetually behind, even when you're doing everything "right." The mind spends an enormous amount of energy suppressing what it knows you are avoiding. This is why people who appear stable on the outside often feel drained on the inside. Suppression is work. Avoidance is effort. Staying put requires more energy than most people realize.

There is also a relational cost. When you don't start the life you feel called toward, parts of you remain hidden. You show up in relationships partially, carefully, filtered through what feels safe. Over time, this creates distance—not necessarily conflict, but disconnection. You may find yourself resenting people who never asked you to shrink, simply because being around them reminds you of what you've postponed. Or you may surround yourself with people who reinforce your hesitation, because their comfort makes your inaction feel justified. Either way, not starting shapes who you feel close to and how deeply you allow yourself to be seen.

Time is another cost, though not in the way people usually think about it. It's not just the passing of years—it's the accumulation of missed feedback. Each year you don't start is a year you don't learn what works, what doesn't, what you enjoy, or what you're capable of handling. You don't gain experience; you gain assumptions. And assumptions harden with age. The longer you wait, the more intimidating starting feels—not because it's harder, but because the gap between where you are and where you imagine you should be grows wider.

Perhaps the most profound cost is **identity erosion**. You begin to define yourself by what you didn't do rather than what you did. You become someone with explanations instead of experiences. Someone who knows why things didn't happen rather than how they unfold. This erosion doesn't happen all at once. It happens slowly, through small accommodations you make to avoid discomfort. But over time, it reshapes how you see yourself. You stop expecting growth. You stop anticipating change. You settle into a version of yourself that feels smaller than it needs to be.

Not starting also distorts how you relate to success in others. When you see someone else doing what you once imagined for yourself, the reaction is rarely pure admiration. It's mixed with comparison, regret, or quiet bitterness. You may dismiss their success as luck, privilege, or timing—not because those factors aren't real, but because acknowledging their courage would force you to confront your own hesitation. This emotional friction is another hidden tax of staying put.

There is a cost to meaning as well. Human beings are not wired to be satisfied by comfort alone. Meaning comes from effort directed toward something that matters. When that effort is absent, life can begin to feel flat, repetitive, or hollow, even when it looks full. You may chase distractions, achievements, or consumption to fill the gap, but the gap remains because it was never about entertainment or status. It was about expression. About becoming more of yourself, not maintaining what already exists.

The most painful cost of not starting is rarely felt in the present—it's felt in hindsight. It arrives in moments when time suddenly becomes visible. When you realize how long you've been saying "someday." When you notice how often you've chosen comfort over courage. When you recognize that the life you've been protecting has quietly been costing you the one you wanted. This realization doesn't come with drama. It comes with a heavy stillness. And it's the moment most people wish they could undo.

This chapter is not meant to frighten you into action. Fear-based urgency creates panic, not progress. It's meant to make the cost visible, because what remains invisible is rarely addressed. Not starting feels safe precisely because its consequences are delayed. But delay does not mean absence. It means accumulation.

You do not need to feel guilty for the time that has passed. Guilt locks you in place just as effectively as fear. What matters is recognizing that staying has a price—and that price is paid whether you acknowledge it or not. The question is not whether you can afford to start. It's whether you can afford not to.

Understanding the cost does not demand immediate action. It simply clarifies the stakes. And once the stakes are clear, waiting no longer feels neutral. It becomes a choice. And choice—real choice—is where the possibility of change finally begins.

Chapter 11

The Small Start That Changes Everything

When most people imagine change, they picture a sweeping transformation—new habits, new routines, a new identity emerging almost overnight. This expectation is not just unrealistic; it's paralyzing. It makes starting feel heavier than it needs to be, as if the first step must somehow contain the weight of the entire journey. But real change rarely begins that way. It begins quietly, with something so small it barely feels like a decision at all.

The small start matters because it works *with* the nervous system, not against it. Large, dramatic actions trigger alarms. They demand certainty, courage, and commitment all at once. Small starts do the opposite. They slip past resistance. They don't ask your brain to rewrite your life; they ask it to tolerate a minor deviation from the familiar. And that tolerance is enough to begin rewiring patterns that have been in place for years.

A small start does not mean a meaningless one. It means an action that is honest, contained, and repeatable. Something that reflects the direction you want to move without demanding proof that you'll succeed. It might be a conversation you've been postponing, not because it will resolve everything, but because it acknowledges what you've been avoiding. It might be setting aside ten minutes to work on something you've told yourself you "don't have time for." It might be allowing yourself to admit, privately, that you want something different—even if you don't yet know what to do about it.

What makes the small start so powerful is that it produces feedback. Until you act, everything lives in your head. Fear remains abstract. Possibility remains hypothetical. The moment you take even a modest step, reality enters the picture. You learn something. Maybe it's not what you expected. Maybe it's harder or easier than you imagined. Either way, you now have information. And information breaks the spell of speculation.

This is where most people misunderstand progress. They believe progress requires visible results. But the earliest progress happens internally. The moment you start, something subtle shifts in how you see yourself. You are no longer someone who only thinks about change—you are someone who has acted. That distinction matters more than the outcome of the action itself. Identity begins to loosen. The story you've been telling yourself starts to crack.

Small starts also change how you relate to fear. Fear thrives on imagination. It grows larger the longer it goes untested. When you act, fear becomes specific. It has boundaries. You realize that discomfort peaks and then subsides. That embarrassment is survivable. That uncertainty does not mean collapse. Each small action teaches your nervous system something it cannot learn through reasoning alone: *I can move and be okay.*

Another overlooked benefit of the small start is that it removes the pressure to be right. When you believe the first step must be perfect, every decision feels high-stakes. Small starts lower the stakes. They allow for adjustment, experimentation, and correction. You are no longer committing to a path; you are exploring a direction. This mindset invites curiosity instead of judgment. You stop asking, *Is this the right choice?* and start asking, *What can I learn from this?*

The simplicity of the small start is often what makes it feel insufficient. It doesn't satisfy the part of you that wants certainty or validation. It doesn't look impressive to others. In fact, it often feels too ordinary to matter. But transformation does not announce itself at the beginning. It accumulates. The most significant changes are often invisible while they are happening.

There is also a discipline to starting small. Not the discipline of intensity, but the discipline of consistency. One small action rarely changes a life. Repeated small actions do. They build momentum quietly. They create a rhythm of movement. Over time, that rhythm becomes familiar. The brain adapts. Resistance lessens. What once felt like effort begins to feel normal. This is how habits form—not through force, but through repetition that the nervous system can tolerate.

The danger at this stage is underestimating what you're doing. You may dismiss your efforts because they don't match the scale of your vision. You may feel tempted to abandon them in search of something more dramatic. This is where many people unknowingly sabotage themselves. They confuse modest beginnings with lack of ambition. In reality, ambition that cannot tolerate small steps rarely survives long enough to become real.

This chapter is not offering a formula. It's offering permission. Permission to begin without certainty. Permission to move without announcing it. Permission to take one step that only you know about. Starting does not require a declaration. It requires a decision—quiet, internal, and often unremarkable.

The small start changes everything because it shifts your relationship with yourself. You begin to trust that movement is possible. You gather evidence instead of excuses. You replace waiting with experimenting. And once that shift occurs, the path forward becomes less about forcing change and more about continuing it.

You do not need to overhaul your life. You do not need to be brave in a way that feels unnatural. You only need to interrupt the pattern of waiting. One honest step is enough to do that. And once the pattern is interrupted, the future no longer feels like something you have to imagine—it becomes something you are actively creating.

Chapter 12
Resistance Will Come Back

One of the most disorienting moments in any journey of change comes after you begin. You take a step—small, honest, real—and for a brief moment, something feels lighter. You feel a sense of relief, maybe even quiet pride. *I did it.* And then, often without warning, resistance returns. Sometimes it comes back stronger than before. This is the point where many people assume they made a mistake. They think, *If this were right, wouldn't it feel easier by now?* The return of resistance feels like betrayal. In reality, it's confirmation. Resistance does not disappear because you start. It adapts.

The mind is remarkably efficient at protecting the status quo. When you take a small step, you introduce a new variable into a system that has been stable for a long time. The brain notices. It recalculates. And when it senses that the old patterns are genuinely being threatened, it escalates its response. What once showed up as mild hesitation may now appear as doubt, fatigue, distraction, or a sudden flood of reasons why this path might not be right after all. This is not regression. It is recalibration.

Most people are unprepared for this phase because they believe starting is the hard part. They assume that once momentum begins, motivation will carry them forward. But motivation is unreliable. It spikes and fades. Resistance, on the other hand, is consistent. It resurfaces precisely when change becomes real. The mistake is interpreting this resurgence as a signal to stop, rather than understanding it as part of the process.

Resistance often changes its voice after you begin. Before starting, it sounds like procrastination. After starting, it sounds like discernment. *Maybe this isn't aligned. Maybe I should rethink this. Maybe there's a better way.* These thoughts feel sophisticated and responsible. They are far more convincing than the initial fear because they are rooted in partial experience. You now know just enough to question yourself without yet knowing enough to feel grounded.

Another common form resistance takes is exhaustion. Not physical exhaustion, but emotional fatigue. Starting requires presence. It asks you to stay engaged with uncertainty, imperfection, and learning curves. This can feel draining, especially if you are accustomed to competence and control. The mind responds by craving relief. Old comforts suddenly feel more tempting. Distractions regain their appeal. The idea of stopping—just for a while—sounds reasonable.

There is also a subtle form of resistance that shows up as self-criticism. You begin evaluating your progress harshly. You compare where you are with where you think you should be. You notice flaws, inefficiencies, and gaps in skill. This inner critique often masquerades as high standards or self-awareness, but its effect is the same: it makes continuing feel heavier than stopping. Perfectionism is rarely about excellence. It is often about avoiding vulnerability.

What's important to understand is that resistance is not a personal flaw—it is a nervous system response to change. Your system has learned to survive in a certain configuration. When you alter that configuration, even slightly, it experiences stress. The stress is not a sign that you are doing harm. It is a sign that the system is adjusting. Just as muscles resist when they are challenged in new ways, your internal patterns resist when they are asked to evolve.

The danger lies in expecting resistance to mean something it doesn't. Many people believe that when resistance appears, it's time to stop and reassess indefinitely. In truth, reassessment has its place, but endless reassessment is simply another form of delay. Growth requires discernment, yes—but it also requires tolerance. Tolerance for discomfort. Tolerance for not knowing. Tolerance for being bad at something before you get better.

Resistance also has a social dimension. As you change, even subtly, the people around you may react. Some will be supportive. Others will feel unsettled, even if they can't articulate why. Your movement disrupts unspoken agreements. It challenges shared narratives about what's possible or acceptable. This can create friction, doubt, or a renewed pull toward the familiar. The temptation to retreat—not because you want to, but because it feels easier—is real.

This is the point where many people stop, not because they can't continue, but because they misinterpret what they're feeling. They assume resistance means they lack discipline or desire. They assume discomfort means misalignment. They assume difficulty means wrong direction. These assumptions are understandable—and incorrect.

The truth is that resistance is part of the rhythm of starting. It comes in waves. It rises when you push into new territory and recedes when you stabilize. It does not require you to fight it or eliminate it. It requires you to recognize it. To say, *This is resistance. This is expected. This does not get to decide for me.*

This chapter is not about pushing harder. It's about staying present. About learning to distinguish between true misalignment and the natural discomfort of growth. About understanding that resistance returning does not erase the progress you've made. It means the change is now real enough to be noticed.

You don't overcome resistance once. You learn how to move with it. You stop waiting for it to disappear and start acting alongside it This is where starting matures—from a single act into a practice. And when you understand that resistance will come back, you stop being surprised by it. You stop being discouraged by it. You stop letting it define the meaning of what you're doing.

Resistance is not the enemy of change. It is the companion that shows up when change is actually happening. And once you stop mistaking its presence for failure, you gain something invaluable: the ability to continue.

Chapter 13

How Identity Quietly Begins to Shift

Identity rarely changes the way people expect it to. There is no moment where you wake up and suddenly feel like a different person. No clear line between who you were and who you are becoming. Instead, identity shifts quietly, almost invisibly, through behavior that contradicts the old story just often enough that the story can no longer hold. This is why so many people miss it while it's happening. They are waiting to *feel* different, not realizing that feeling different is the last thing to arrive.

For most of your life, identity has felt fixed. You've described yourself in familiar ways—responsible, cautious, practical, creative but realistic, ambitious but grounded. These labels were not chosen randomly. They were shaped by repetition. You did certain things consistently, avoided others consistently, and over time your mind drew conclusions. *This is who I am. This is what I do. This is what I don't.* Identity, at its core, is simply the brain's attempt to create a coherent narrative out of repeated behavior.

This is why thinking alone never changes who you are. You can imagine a different life, visualize a different version of yourself, even believe in your potential—and still remain exactly the same. Thought does not threaten identity. Action does. The moment you behave in a way that doesn't fit the old narrative, the system is forced to respond. At first, it resists. It tells you that the behavior was an exception, a fluke, a one-time thing. *That wasn't really you.* But when the behavior repeats, the story begins to weaken.

This is how identity begins to shift—not through declarations, but through evidence.

At the beginning, the evidence feels fragile. You may take a small step and immediately downplay it. *That doesn't count. Anyone could do that. It's not enough to mean anything.* This minimization is not humility; it is the old identity protecting itself. If the action doesn't count, the story doesn't have to change. The mind would rather discredit the behavior than rewrite the self. But the evidence accumulates anyway.

You start noticing small changes in how you respond to situations. You speak up where you would have stayed quiet. You try again where you would have quit. You tolerate uncertainty a little longer than before. These shifts don't feel heroic. In fact, they often feel awkward and unsteady. But they matter because they are inconsistent with who you used to believe you were.

This is where identity friction emerges. Part of you still sees yourself through the old lens, while another part begins to recognize new behavior. This friction can feel disorienting. You may feel like you're pretending, or that you don't quite belong in the new space you're stepping into. This sensation is often mislabeled as imposter syndrome. In reality, it is identity catching up to action. You are behaving like someone new before you feel like them.

The mind hates this lag. It prefers alignment between self-image and behavior. When they don't match, discomfort arises. The temptation is to resolve the discomfort by reverting to old behavior—because that's easier than updating the identity. This is why early change feels unstable. You are in between versions of yourself. You no longer fully fit the old story, but you don't yet trust the new one.

What most people don't realize is that this in-between state is not a problem. It is the process.

Identity does not leap forward; it inches forward. It updates slowly, conservatively, based on patterns it can no longer ignore. One action does not redefine you. Ten similar actions begin to. Fifty make it undeniable. Eventually, something shifts. You hear yourself say, *I'm the kind of person who follows through.* Or, *I don't avoid these conversations anymore.* Or simply, *I start things.* The statement doesn't feel dramatic—it feels factual. And that's how you know identity has changed.

This shift is powerful because it changes how effort feels. When action aligns with identity, resistance decreases. You no longer need to convince yourself to move; movement feels congruent. This doesn't mean things become easy. It means they become less internally conflicted. You stop fighting yourself at every step. Energy that was once spent negotiating is now available for learning and adapting.

Another subtle change occurs in how you relate to setbacks. When identity is fragile, setbacks feel personal. They threaten the story you're trying to build. When identity is grounded in behavior rather than outcomes, setbacks feel informative. They don't erase who you are becoming; they refine it. You no longer interpret difficulty as evidence you shouldn't be here. You interpret it as part of being here.

Relationships often shift during this phase as well. Not always dramatically, but noticeably. You may find that certain conversations no longer resonate. Certain dynamics feel constricting. This can be unsettling, especially if your old identity was tied to being agreeable, dependable, or predictable. As identity evolves, alignment becomes more important than approval. This doesn't mean you become reckless or insensitive—it means you become more honest about who you are and what you need.

There is also a quiet strengthening of self-trust that begins to take root. Not the loud confidence often portrayed in media, but a steadier sense of internal reliability. You begin to believe yourself when you say you'll do something. You stop overpromising and underdelivering. You choose smaller commitments you can keep, and each kept commitment reinforces the new identity. Trust builds not through intention, but through follow-through.

This chapter matters because identity is the long game. Motivation fades. Circumstances change. Emotions fluctuate. Identity endures. When you become someone who starts— who moves before clarity, who acts despite discomfort—the behavior no longer feels extraordinary. It feels normal. And what feels normal is sustainable.

The shift will not announce itself. There will be no ceremony. One day, you will simply realize that the questions you used to ask no longer dominate your thinking. You don't spend as much time debating whether you're allowed to begin. You spend more time engaging with what's in front of you. The old hesitation hasn't vanished, but it no longer runs the show.

Identity doesn't change because you decided to change. It changes because you behaved differently long enough that the old story could no longer survive. And once that happens, starting is no longer something you try to do. It becomes part of who you are.

Chapter 14

Why Momentum Feels Fragile

Momentum is one of the most misunderstood forces in personal change. People talk about it as if it's something you either have or don't have—an invisible wind at your back that suddenly appears and carries you forward. When it fades, they assume something went wrong. *I lost momentum. I broke the streak. I'm back at square one.* This interpretation is not only inaccurate; it's one of the fastest ways to sabotage real progress.

Momentum feels fragile because, in its early stages, it is quiet and easily disrupted. It hasn't yet solidified into habit or identity. It lives in repetition that still requires intention. At this stage, missing a day, hesitating on a step, or feeling uncertain can feel catastrophic. You mistake interruption for failure. In reality, early momentum is not meant to feel strong—it is meant to feel *deliberate*.

The belief that momentum should feel effortless is another leftover myth. Effortlessness comes later, after patterns stabilize. In the beginning, momentum feels like remembering to choose again. It feels like recommitting without drama. It feels like doing the thing even when the emotional reward hasn't caught up yet. This is why people often assume they're doing it wrong. They expect momentum to remove friction, when its real job is to teach you how to move *with* friction.

One reason momentum feels so unstable is that it is not linear. Progress does not move in a straight line; it moves in waves. There are days when energy is high and clarity feels close. There are other days when doubt resurfaces and the old identity tries to reclaim control. These fluctuations are normal, but they clash with the expectation that once you start, things should continuously improve. When reality doesn't match that expectation, discouragement sets in.

Another contributor to fragile momentum is over-identification with short-term outcomes. You take a step and look immediately for results. When they don't appear—or appear more slowly than expected—you interpret that delay as evidence that the effort isn't working. This is where many people stop, not because progress isn't happening, but because it hasn't become visible yet. Momentum often builds internally long before it shows up externally. Neural pathways, emotional tolerance, and identity alignment are shifting beneath the surface, even when circumstances look unchanged.

There is also a subtle pressure that accompanies early momentum: the pressure to *maintain* it perfectly. You become hyper-aware of your behavior. You monitor yourself constantly. You worry that one misstep will erase everything you've built. This creates tension, and tension is exhausting. Momentum does not thrive under constant surveillance. It thrives under rhythm.

Real momentum is not about intensity; it is about consistency that can survive imperfection. It is built through actions that are small enough to repeat even on low-energy days. This is why grand routines often collapse while modest ones endure. The nervous system prefers predictability over ambition. When a behavior feels manageable, it becomes repeatable. When it becomes repeatable, it becomes automatic. That is when momentum stops feeling fragile and starts feeling stable.

Another overlooked factor is emotional recovery. Momentum falters not because people stop moving, but because they don't know how to return after a pause. They treat interruption as failure rather than as a natural part of the process. The ability to resume—without shame, self-criticism, or overcorrection—is what actually sustains momentum over time. The people who change their lives are not those who never stop; they are those who know how to restart quickly.

Momentum also strengthens when you shift what you measure. Instead of tracking outcomes, you track engagement. *Did I show up? Did I take a step? Did I respond rather than avoid?* These metrics are within your control. They reinforce identity rather than performance. When momentum is tied to identity—*I am someone who continues*—it becomes far more resilient than when it is tied to results.

There is a moment, often unnoticed, when momentum crosses a threshold. The action no longer feels like a decision. You don't debate whether to do it; you simply do it. The energy required decreases. The resistance softens. What once felt fragile now feels familiar. This is not because you became stronger overnight, but because the behavior became integrated. The system adapted.

What's important to understand is that momentum does not build by protecting it from disruption. It builds by surviving disruption. Each time you pause and return, you reinforce the belief that movement is possible even when conditions aren't perfect. This belief is far more valuable than uninterrupted streaks. It creates durability.

This chapter is meant to reframe how you relate to momentum. Not as something to chase or guard anxiously, but as something that grows through patience and repetition. You don't need to feel unstoppable. You need to feel willing to continue. The difference matters.

Momentum is not a rush of energy. It is trust built through repetition. It is the quiet confidence that even if you slow down, even if you hesitate, even if you doubt—you know how to begin again. And once you know that, momentum stops feeling fragile. It becomes part of how you move through life.

Chapter 15
Why Discipline Fails

Discipline is often treated as the ultimate solution. When people struggle to start, to continue, or to follow through, the diagnosis comes quickly: *You just need more discipline.* The prescription sounds simple, almost moral. Try harder. Push through. Be stronger than your excuses. And for a short time, this approach may even work. You grit your teeth, summon willpower, and force yourself forward. But eventually—often sooner than you'd like—it collapses. The routine breaks. The effort fades. And you're left wondering why something that was supposed to be the answer keeps failing you.

The problem is not that discipline is useless. It's that discipline is a limited resource, and most people are trying to use it as a foundation instead of a supplement. Discipline works best in short bursts, in contained environments, and for clearly defined tasks. It was never meant to carry the full weight of long-term personal change. When you rely on discipline alone, you are asking your conscious mind to overpower habits, identity, nervous system wiring, and emotional patterns that were built over years. That is not strength—that is exhaustion waiting to happen.

Discipline fails because it treats resistance as an enemy to be defeated rather than a signal to be understood. It frames change as a battle between the "good" part of you that wants growth and the "bad" part that wants comfort. This internal war creates tension, and tension is unsustainable. You may win for a while, but eventually the part of you that is tired, overwhelmed, or seeking relief will reclaim control. When it does, the fallout often includes guilt, self-criticism, and the familiar conclusion: *I just don't have what it takes.*

What discipline-based change overlooks is context. Human behavior does not happen in a vacuum. It happens within environments, routines, emotional states, and social systems. When those factors are ignored, discipline becomes a constant uphill climb. You're fighting friction at every step. The effort required to maintain momentum becomes so high that stopping feels like relief. This is why so many people cycle between intense effort and complete disengagement. It's not a lack of character—it's a flawed strategy.

Another reason discipline fails is that it depends heavily on motivation, even if it pretends not to. Discipline is easier when motivation is high and far harder when it's low. But motivation fluctuates. It responds to sleep, stress, mood, and circumstance. Building a life on something so unstable guarantees inconsistency. When motivation dips, discipline is forced to compensate. When discipline is forced too often, burnout follows.

There is also an identity cost to relying solely on discipline. When progress is framed as something you must constantly force yourself to do, it reinforces the belief that growth is unnatural for you. You begin to see yourself as someone who has to fight to improve, rather than someone who is capable of evolving. This subtle narrative matters. Over time, it shapes how you approach challenges, setbacks, and even success.

For readers who value discipline, structure, and grit, this idea can feel uncomfortable—almost irresponsible. But the limitation of discipline is not a matter of character; it is a matter of biology.

Research in psychology has repeatedly shown that willpower is a finite resource, not an endless one. In their seminal work on ego depletion, Roy Baumeister and his colleagues demonstrated that sustained self-control draws from a limited mental reserve, which becomes depleted under stress, fatigue, or prolonged effort (Baumeister et al., 1998). When that reserve runs low, people don't fail because they are weak—they fail because the system is overloaded.

This is why discipline-heavy approaches often work temporarily and then collapse. They demand constant resistance against the brain's drive for efficiency and safety. Over time, this creates burnout, resentment, and self-blame—not progress.

What works better is not abandoning discipline, but relocating it. Discipline becomes sustainable when it is applied to designing environments, routines, and commitments that reduce friction instead of increasing pressure. In this way, discipline supports momentum rather than trying to manufacture it.

What replaces discipline is not laziness or lack of structure. It is **design**.

Design works with human behavior instead of against it. It acknowledges that you are not a machine and stops expecting you to operate like one. Instead of asking, *How do I force myself to do this?* design asks, *How do I make this easier to continue?* It shifts the focus from willpower to environment, from intensity to sustainability, from control to alignment.

Design starts by reducing friction rather than increasing effort. Small changes in your environment—physical, digital, and social—can dramatically alter behavior without requiring constant discipline. When the right action is the easiest action, consistency follows naturally. This is not a trick; it's an acknowledgment of how humans actually operate.

Another element that replaces discipline is **identity alignment**. When actions align with who you believe yourself to be, they require far less effort. You don't need discipline to brush your teeth because it fits your identity. You don't debate it; you do it. The same principle applies to growth. When starting, continuing, and adapting become part of how you see yourself, the behavior stops feeling forced. It becomes expected.

Compassion also plays a critical role. Discipline often comes bundled with harsh self-talk—*no excuses, push harder, don't be weak*. Compassion, by contrast, allows for recovery without collapse. It creates space to pause and return without turning interruption into failure. This does not lower standards; it stabilizes them. People who change sustainably are not those who punish themselves into progress, but those who know how to re-engage without shame.

Structure replaces discipline as well, but not rigid structure. Flexible structure. Rhythms instead of rules. Patterns that can bend without breaking. This kind of structure anticipates fluctuation. It expects low-energy days and makes room for them. Instead of demanding the same output regardless of circumstance, it preserves continuity. Something small still gets done. The chain doesn't break completely.

Perhaps most importantly, meaning replaces discipline. Discipline relies on pressure. Meaning relies on connection. When an action is tied to something you genuinely care about—something that reflects who you are becoming—it draws you forward rather than pushing you from behind. This doesn't eliminate resistance, but it changes your relationship with it. You tolerate discomfort more easily when you understand why you're enduring it.

This chapter is not an argument against effort. Effort matters. But effort that is unsupported by design, identity, compassion, and meaning will always be fragile. Discipline can get you started in moments of urgency. It cannot carry you through seasons of change.

The people who build lives they're proud of are not the most disciplined. They are the most aligned. They stop trying to overpower themselves and start creating conditions where growth is the natural outcome. When you understand this, the question shifts. It's no longer, *How do I force myself to keep going?* It becomes, *How do I set my life up so continuing makes sense?*

And when continuing makes sense, discipline becomes optional. Movement becomes normal. And starting—once the hardest part—becomes something you know how to return to, again and again. This kind of alignment doesn't lower standards, it quietly raises them.

Key Reference

- Baumeister, R. F., et al. (1998). Ego Depletion: Is the Active Self a Limited Resource? *Journal of Personality and Social Psychology.*

Chapter 16

Starting in the Middle of a Life You Can't Walk Away From

One of the quiet reasons people don't start is that they believe starting requires escape. Escape from responsibilities. Escape from commitments. Escape from the life they already built. The fantasy goes something like this: *If I could just get away for a while... if I didn't have so many obligations... if I could hit reset.* This belief is understandable—and paralyzing—because most people cannot walk away from their lives. They have families, mortgages, careers, histories, and people who depend on them. When starting is framed as leaving, it becomes impossible before it even begins.

The truth is less dramatic and far more realistic: most meaningful change begins in the middle, not at the edge. It starts while you are still showing up to work, still caring for others, still honoring commitments you cannot simply abandon. This reality frustrates people because it strips away the clean narrative of reinvention. There is no blank slate. There is only the life you have and the direction you choose to move within it.

Starting in the middle feels messy because it requires integration rather than replacement. You are not trading one life for another—you are layering something new onto what already exists. This creates tension. Time feels scarce. Energy feels divided. Progress feels slower than you hoped. The temptation is to conclude that now isn't the right moment, that starting under these conditions will never work. But these conditions are not a barrier—they are the context in which real change happens.

One of the most difficult adjustments is accepting that starting will initially *add* complexity rather than reduce it. There is a brief period where you carry both the old and the new. Old routines still demand attention while new ones require energy. This overlap can feel overwhelming, especially for people who value order and control. The mind looks for relief and offers a familiar solution: wait until things calm down. The problem is that things rarely calm down on their own. Waiting becomes a way of outsourcing change to a future that never quite arrives.

Starting in the middle also challenges perfectionism. You don't have ideal conditions. You can't give the new pursuit your full focus. You will make progress in fragments. This can feel unsatisfying, even discouraging. But fragmented progress is still progress. In fact, it is often more sustainable because it forces you to build change into real life rather than a fantasy version of it. What you can do consistently under imperfect conditions is what will last.

There is also an emotional challenge to starting without escape: you must tolerate being misunderstood. From the outside, your efforts may look unfocused or unnecessary. People may question why you're adding something new when you already seem busy enough. They may interpret your starting as restlessness or dissatisfaction with what you have. This can trigger guilt, especially if you pride yourself on being dependable. Learning to hold both gratitude for your current life and desire for something more is uncomfortable—but essential.

Another hidden difficulty is confronting the belief that starting late or slowly makes it less legitimate. You may compare yourself to people who appear all-in, who seem to have more freedom, fewer constraints, or earlier starts. This comparison is rarely fair. Everyone's starting point is different. Starting in the middle requires a different kind of courage— not the courage to leap, but the courage to persist quietly without external validation.

What makes starting in the middle powerful is that it grounds change in reality. You don't get to reinvent yourself in isolation; you get to evolve within your actual circumstances. This forces clarity. You learn quickly what matters enough to make room for. You discover which commitments support your growth and which quietly drain it. The process refines your priorities not through reflection alone, but through lived experience.

There is also a deep dignity in this kind of starting. It honors what you've built rather than dismissing it. It acknowledges that your past choices were made with the information and capacity you had at the time. You are not rejecting your life— you are expanding it. This perspective reduces internal conflict. You stop framing change as betrayal and start framing it as continuation.

Starting in the middle teaches patience. Results come slower, but they are sturdier. Each step is integrated into the fabric of your life. You don't have to maintain a separate version of yourself for the dream and the day-to-day. Over time, the two begin to inform each other. The life you're building feeds the life you're living, and vice versa.

This chapter matters because most people will never have the luxury of a clean break. Waiting for one is another form of postponement. The question is not whether you can start under perfect conditions. It's whether you are willing to start under real ones. Real conditions include fatigue, uncertainty, competing demands, and imperfect focus. They also include resilience, adaptability, and a depth of experience you didn't have before.

You don't need to leave your life to begin. You need to begin within it. Change does not require disappearance. It requires integration. And once you understand that starting is something you do alongside your existing commitments—not instead of them—the path forward becomes not only possible, but practical.

Starting in the middle is not a compromise. It is how most meaningful lives are actually built.

Chapter 17

Why Waiting for Permission Keeps You Trapped

Most people don't realize they're waiting for permission. They would never say it out loud. They see themselves as independent, capable, and self-directed. And yet, beneath the surface, there is a quiet pause that governs their choices—a hesitation that sounds like caution, but feels more like standing in line for approval that never arrives. Permission, when unexamined, becomes one of the most powerful invisible forces keeping people exactly where they are.

Permission doesn't always come from a single authority figure. Sometimes it comes from parents whose voices still echo long after childhood. Sometimes it comes from employers, partners, cultural norms, or unspoken expectations about what someone "like you" is allowed to want. More often than not, permission comes from an imagined audience—people whose opinions you anticipate, project, and internalize without ever hearing them directly. You wait not because someone told you no, but because no one explicitly told you yes.

This pattern begins early. As children, permission is necessary for survival. We are taught to ask before acting, to seek approval before making decisions, to follow rules to stay safe and accepted. Over time, this external permission becomes internalized. You learn that initiative without approval can lead to punishment, rejection, or loss of belonging. The lesson sticks, even when the environment changes. As an adult, the stakes are different—but the wiring remains.

Waiting for permission feels responsible. It feels respectful. It feels mature. You tell yourself you're being considerate, thoughtful, measured. But what often lies beneath that restraint is fear—fear of disapproval, fear of judgment, fear of being seen as selfish, reckless, or naive. Permission becomes a shield. If someone else approves your decision, then the risk is shared. If they don't, you don't have to act at all.

This is why permission is so seductive. It offers safety without progress. As long as you're waiting, you're not failing. You're not wrong. You're just "not there yet." The problem is that permission is rarely given for things that challenge the status quo. People are comfortable approving what already makes sense to them. They are far less comfortable endorsing paths they don't understand or wouldn't choose for themselves. When you wait for permission to start something meaningful, you're often asking people invested in your stability to approve your disruption.

Another reason permission keeps people trapped is that it delays ownership. As long as you're waiting for someone else to validate your desire, you don't have to fully commit to it yourself. You can keep the dream at arm's length, protected from scrutiny and accountability. Permission allows you to remain undecided while appearing cautious. But indecision has a cost. Over time, waiting erodes confidence. You begin to doubt your instincts, your timing, your right to choose.

There is also a hidden grief tied to permission-seeking. Every time you defer your own authority, you reinforce the belief that your desires are conditional. That they must be justified, approved, or earned. This belief quietly shapes how you move through the world. You second-guess yourself. You over-explain. You look outward for answers that can only come from within. And slowly, the voice that knows what you want becomes harder to hear.

Permission is especially dangerous when it disguises itself as consensus. You tell yourself you'll start once everyone is on board. Once it makes sense to the people you care about. Once there's no friction. But meaningful change almost always creates friction. If you wait until your path is universally understood, you will wait forever. Growth does not require agreement. It requires alignment.

This chapter is not suggesting that you ignore wisdom, advice, or collaboration. Discernment matters. Listening matters. But there is a difference between seeking perspective and outsourcing authority. Advice should inform your decision, not replace it. When you defer the final say to others, you give away something essential—the right to shape your own life.

What most people eventually realize is that permission is not something you receive. It is something you claim. And claiming it does not require confrontation or rebellion. It requires acceptance. Acceptance that not everyone will understand. Acceptance that some people may disagree. Acceptance that approval is not guaranteed—and that it doesn't have to be.

The moment you stop waiting for permission, something subtle shifts. You stop asking whether you're allowed to begin and start asking whether you're willing to. You recognize that your life is already in motion, whether you act or not. That time is already passing. That choosing not to choose is still a choice—just one made by default rather than intention.

Waiting for permission feels safer than taking responsibility. But safety without ownership is another form of confinement. When you give yourself permission to start—quietly, imperfectly, without consensus—you step into authorship. You stop living as a respondent to expectations and begin living as a participant in your own direction.

No one is coming to authorize your life. No one will hand you a certificate saying you're ready, worthy, or allowed. That moment never arrives because it was never meant to come from outside you. Permission is not granted. It is assumed.

And once you assume it, starting is no longer a question of whether you're allowed—it becomes a question of whether you're willing to live with the consequences of choosing yourself.

Chapter 18

The Fear That Looks Like Logic

Fear rarely announces itself as fear. If it did, most people would recognize it and question it. Instead, fear disguises itself as reason. It sounds calm, measured, intelligent. It uses evidence, probabilities, and hypotheticals. It speaks in full sentences and makes compelling arguments. This is why it's so effective. When fear wears the mask of logic, it doesn't feel like something to overcome—it feels like something to obey.

This version of fear doesn't shout. It explains. It presents spreadsheets, timelines, and contingency plans. It asks thoughtful questions like, *Is this sustainable? What's the downside? What if this doesn't work?* These questions are not inherently wrong. In fact, they are often useful. The problem arises when they are used not to refine action, but to delay it indefinitely. Logic becomes a tool not for movement, but for avoidance.

The mind is exceptionally skilled at constructing airtight cases for staying exactly where you are. It can list every reason why starting now is premature, irresponsible, or unnecessary. It can pull examples from the past, stories from others, and statistics from the world at large. The argument always ends the same way: *Waiting makes sense.* And because the reasoning feels sound, you rarely question the conclusion.

What goes unnoticed is that logic, in this context, is not neutral. It is being selectively applied. The mind scrutinizes the risks of starting while ignoring the risks of staying. It demands certainty for movement but accepts ambiguity for stagnation. It asks for proof that change will work but never asks for proof that continuing will lead to fulfillment. This imbalance is not accidental—it is protective.

Fear prefers the known, even when the known is unsatisfying. Logic becomes its ally by framing the familiar as the safer option. The longer you stay, the more data you accumulate about why leaving would be difficult. The more difficult it seems, the more justified staying feels. Over time, this loop reinforces itself. Fear doesn't have to convince you to stop—it only has to convince you to wait.

Another reason fear hides behind logic is that logic provides moral cover. It allows you to feel responsible rather than afraid. You can tell yourself you're not avoiding action—you're being smart. You're not hesitating—you're being strategic. This self-image matters, especially for people who value competence and thoughtfulness. Admitting fear would challenge that identity. Rationalizing delay preserves it.

This is particularly true when starting would disrupt an image you've worked hard to maintain. Logic becomes the gatekeeper that protects reputation, consistency, and predictability. It keeps you aligned with expectations. It prevents embarrassment. It avoids explanations you're not ready to give. All of this can be framed as prudence, even when the underlying driver is fear of exposure.

The danger of fear disguised as logic is that it rarely feels urgent. There is no alarm bell. There is no crisis. You simply keep deciding to wait. Days turn into months. Months turn into years. Each decision feels reasonable in isolation. The cost only becomes visible in hindsight, when you realize how long you've been standing still.

Another subtle effect of this pattern is that it erodes intuition. When logic is always given the final say, the quieter signals—the ones that speak through restlessness, curiosity, or longing—are dismissed. You stop trusting what you feel unless you can justify it intellectually. Over time, the ability to listen inward weakens. You become fluent in analysis and disconnected from desire.

This chapter is not arguing against thinking carefully. Thought matters. Planning matters. Discernment matters. But logic is meant to support action, not replace it. When logic becomes a prerequisite for movement rather than a companion to it, it stops serving you. It becomes a cage with very convincing walls.

The shift begins when you start asking different questions. Instead of asking, *Is this guaranteed?* you ask, *What would I learn if I tried?* Instead of asking, *What could go wrong?* you ask, *What happens if I never begin?* These questions don't eliminate fear, but they rebalance the conversation. They allow logic to inform action rather than veto it.

Fear loses its grip when it is named. When you recognize that the argument keeping you still is not purely rational, but protective, something changes. You don't have to silence the fear. You simply stop mistaking it for truth. You acknowledge its concern without surrendering your agency.

This chapter matters because many people believe they are stuck due to circumstances or complexity, when in reality they are stuck in a conversation that has been looping for years. Fear has been speaking in the language of reason, and reason has been trusted without question.

Starting does not require abandoning logic. It requires refusing to let logic be used exclusively in service of staying the same. When you allow logic and courage to work together— one informing the other rather than overpowering it—you create space for movement that is both thoughtful and alive.

Fear may still speak. Logic may still question. But neither gets to decide alone. And in that balance, starting becomes possible again.

Chapter 19
When the Dream Changes

One of the quiet fears that keeps people from starting is the belief that once they begin, they will be locked in. That choosing a direction means committing to it forever. That if the dream shifts, evolves, or even dissolves, it will somehow invalidate the effort that came before. This belief creates a dangerous rigidity. It convinces people that they must get it right the first time, because changing their mind later would mean admitting they were wrong. And so, instead of risking adjustment, they choose stasis.

But dreams are not contracts. They are conversations.

What you want at one stage of your life is shaped by who you are at that moment—your experiences, wounds, responsibilities, and hopes. As you grow, your perspective changes. Your values refine. Your understanding deepens. It would be unnatural for your dream not to change along with you. Expecting a vision to remain static while you evolve is like expecting a child to keep wearing the same clothes year after year. Growth demands revision.

This is why starting is so important. Not because it guarantees you'll arrive where you thought you were going, but because it reveals where you actually belong. Movement provides information that thinking never can. Once you begin, you encounter reality—your energy, your interests, your tolerance for certain sacrifices, your appetite for risk. Some parts of the dream light you up more than expected. Others feel hollow once experienced. This is not disappointment. It is clarity earned through engagement.

Many people interpret this shift as failure. *I thought I wanted this, but now I'm not so sure.* They judge themselves for changing direction, believing it proves they were misguided, impulsive, or unrealistic. In truth, it proves the opposite. It proves they were willing to learn. It proves they were listening. It proves they were alive to the process instead of clinging to an idea out of pride.

The only dreams that never change are the ones that never meet reality.

There is a particular kind of shame that can surface when a dream evolves. You may worry about how it looks to others. You may fear being labeled inconsistent, unfocused, or unreliable. This fear is often rooted in a misunderstanding of commitment. Commitment is not loyalty to a fixed outcome;

it is loyalty to growth. When you continue down a path that no longer aligns simply to avoid changing course, you are not being committed—you are being attached.

Attachment to a dream can be just as limiting as fear of starting. It keeps you loyal to an identity that no longer fits. It pressures you to justify past effort rather than respond to present truth. The sunk cost fallacy—continuing something because you've already invested time or energy—shows up here as emotional obligation. *I've already come this far. I can't stop now.* But progress is not measured by how long you stay—it's measured by how honestly you respond to what you learn.

Another reason changing dreams feels threatening is that it disrupts narrative coherence. We like clean stories. We like to explain our lives in a way that makes sense. When a dream changes, the story becomes messier. It includes pivots, pauses, and detours. But real lives are not linear. They are layered. The attempt to force a tidy narrative often costs people their authenticity.

What most people don't realize is that evolving dreams are a sign of integrity. They indicate that you are paying attention. That you are letting experience inform direction. That you are willing to let go of what no longer serves you, even when it once mattered deeply. This requires courage. It is far easier to cling to an outdated vision than to admit you've outgrown it.

There is also a quiet liberation in allowing the dream to change. The pressure to "make it work" eases. You stop trying to force alignment where it doesn't exist. You begin asking better questions. *What part of this still matters? What am I learning about myself? What direction feels more honest now?* These questions don't erase the past—they integrate it.

Starting teaches you something essential: that movement is not about arriving at a final destination. It is about staying responsive. The person who starts and adjusts is not indecisive; they are adaptive. They are in conversation with their own becoming. They understand that life is not a straight line to a fixed goal, but a series of informed choices made in real time.

This chapter matters because many people never start out of fear that they might change their mind. They treat that possibility as evidence of weakness rather than wisdom. In reality, refusing to start because the dream might evolve is like refusing to speak because your opinion might deepen. Growth always involves revision.

You are allowed to change. You are allowed to refine. You are allowed to discover that what you thought you wanted was only a doorway to something truer. None of that erases the value of starting. It validates it.

A dream that changes does not mean you failed. It means you listened. And listening—to yourself, to reality, to what life is teaching you—is one of the clearest signs that you are no longer stuck.

Starting does not bind you. It frees you to learn.

Chapter 20

The Quiet Confidence That Comes After Starting

There is a kind of confidence most people chase their entire lives, and rarely find. It's loud, polished, and performative. It shows up as certainty, charisma, and the ability to speak convincingly about where you're going and why. This is the confidence we see celebrated—on stages, in interviews, across social media. And because it looks impressive, people assume it must come first. That they need to *feel* confident before they act. What they don't see is the quieter confidence that forms underneath all of that—the kind that only arrives *after* starting.

This confidence does not announce itself. It doesn't change how you talk overnight or make you immune to doubt. In fact, you may not recognize it at first. It shows up subtly, in how you respond to challenges, how you recover from missteps, and how you relate to uncertainty. It is not the absence of fear—it is the absence of paralysis. It is the calm knowing that even if things don't go as planned, you will figure it out because you already have.

Quiet confidence is built from experience, not affirmation. Every time you take a step and survive it, something shifts. Your nervous system updates its expectations. What once felt threatening becomes manageable. What once required emotional effort becomes routine. This is not because the world suddenly becomes safer, but because you become more capable within it. Confidence, in this sense, is not belief—it is memory. The memory that you've faced uncertainty before and remained intact.

This is why confidence gained through starting is fundamentally different from confidence borrowed through motivation or encouragement. External validation can inspire you temporarily, but it does not anchor you. When things get difficult—and they will—you don't fall back on slogans or reassurance. You fall back on lived evidence. *I've handled this before. I can handle it again.* That thought carries weight because it's earned.

Another way this quiet confidence reveals itself is through restraint. You feel less compelled to prove yourself. Less reactive to criticism or comparison. When you haven't started, other people's opinions carry disproportionate power because you are still trying to determine who you are. Once you've begun moving, your sense of self becomes more grounded.

You don't need everyone to understand your choices. You don't need constant feedback. You are oriented inward, guided by experience rather than speculation.

This confidence also changes how you approach problems. Before starting, obstacles feel like stop signs. They confirm your fears and reinforce hesitation. After starting, obstacles become data. You still feel frustration, but it's contextual. You ask different questions. *What's missing? What needs adjustment? What did this teach me?* The emotional charge softens. You engage rather than retreat.

One of the most surprising effects of this confidence is how it reshapes patience. You stop expecting instant clarity or dramatic breakthroughs. You understand that progress unfolds unevenly. This patience is not passive—it's grounded. It comes from knowing that momentum is built through repetition, not intensity. You don't rush yourself because you're no longer trying to outrun doubt. You're building something real.

Quiet confidence also affects how you relate to the future. You stop trying to predict every outcome. Not because you don't care, but because you trust your ability to adapt. Planning becomes flexible. Goals become directional rather than rigid. The future no longer feels like something you must control— it feels like something you can engage with. This shift reduces anxiety and increases agency at the same time.

What's important to understand is that this confidence does not arrive all at once. It accumulates. It grows through small wins, honest failures, and continued participation. Some days you'll feel it clearly. Other days it will sit quietly in the background, unnoticed. But over time, it becomes part of how you carry yourself. You stop asking, *Am I capable?* and start asking, *What's next?*

This chapter matters because many people believe confidence is the reward for success. In reality, confidence is the byproduct of engagement. You don't earn it by being right—you earn it by staying involved. By continuing when things are unclear. By adjusting instead of abandoning. By starting again when momentum slows.

The irony is that once this confidence forms, it often looks effortless from the outside. People may tell you that you're brave, decisive, or naturally confident. They don't see the quiet accumulation of moments that built it. They don't see the small starts, the uncertainty, the early discomfort. They see the result, not the process.

And that's okay. This confidence was never meant to be performed. It was meant to support you. To give you a stable center from which to keep moving, learning, and choosing. It doesn't promise success. It promises resilience. And resilience is what allows starting to become a way of life, not a one-time event.

You don't start because you're confident. You become confident because you started—and kept going.

Chapter 21
When the Old Life Starts Pulling You Back

There is a moment that almost no one talks about, yet nearly everyone experiences it. You've started. Not dramatically, not perfectly, but honestly. You've taken steps. You've felt the subtle shift in identity, the quiet confidence beginning to form. And then—often when you least expect it—the old life reaches for you. Not aggressively. Not with force. But gently. Familiar routines resurface. Old comforts regain their appeal. The version of you that knows how to survive without stretching whispers, *Come back. It was easier here.*

This pull is not failure. It is gravity.

The life you've lived up to this point has momentum of its own. Habits, relationships, expectations, and self-perceptions do not disappear just because you've chosen a new direction. They continue to exert influence, not out of malice, but out of familiarity. The old life knows you. It knows how to reward you quickly—with comfort, approval, predictability. The new life, by contrast, is still asking something of you. Presence. Uncertainty. Patience. When energy dips or stress rises, the pull backward can feel almost irresistible.

This is where many people quietly stop. Not because they don't care anymore, but because returning feels like relief. The old routines require less attention. The old roles fit without effort. You can move through them on autopilot. The nervous system relaxes. And in that moment of relief, it's easy to tell yourself that starting was just a phase. That maybe you were overthinking things. That perhaps this—what you already have—is enough.

The danger is not the pull itself. The danger is mistaking comfort for truth.

The old life pulls hardest when the new one hasn't yet delivered visible results. When effort outweighs reward. When you're doing the work but not yet seeing the payoff. This gap—between initiation and evidence—is where doubt thrives. The mind looks for certainty and finds it in the familiar. *At least here I know who I am.* The question becomes not whether the old life fits, but whether you're willing to tolerate the discomfort of becoming.

Another layer of this pull comes from other people. As you change, even subtly, the dynamics around you shift. Some people will encourage you. Others will unconsciously invite you back into old patterns. They may not even realize they're doing it. They miss the version of you that was predictable, available, or aligned with their expectations. Their comfort with who you were can feel like validation when you're tired or uncertain.

This is where clarity matters. The pull back does not mean you were wrong to start. It means you are in transition. Every meaningful change includes a period where the old life still feels close enough to reach, while the new life is not yet fully formed. This in-between space is uncomfortable precisely because it asks you to choose without reinforcement. To continue without applause. To trust something you are still building.

What makes this phase particularly challenging is that the old life often offers reasonable arguments. *Why make things harder? Why disrupt what works? Why keep pushing when you could just settle back in?* These questions are not irrational. They are rooted in self-preservation. But preservation and growth are not the same thing. One maintains what exists. The other requires letting it loosen its grip.

There is grief here, even if it's subtle. You may grieve the ease of the old routines, the simplicity of not having to question yourself, the comfort of being known in a certain way. Acknowledging this grief matters. Pretending you don't miss aspects of your old life only gives them more power. When you name what you're leaving behind, you reclaim choice instead of reacting unconsciously.

This chapter is not asking you to reject your past or demonize your old life. It served you. It got you here. But what got you here is not obligated to take you where you're going. The pull backward is not a command—it's an invitation. You get to decide whether to accept it.

The key is not to fight the pull, but to understand it. To recognize that longing for familiarity does not negate your desire for growth. Both can coexist. You can appreciate what was while still choosing what's next. The mistake is believing you must resolve that tension before moving forward. You don't. You move forward *with* it.

When the old life pulls, the question is not *Why am I feeling this?* The question is *What am I being asked to choose right now?* Comfort or continuation. Familiarity or alignment. Ease or expansion. None of these choices make you a better or worse person. But only one moves you forward.

The old life will always be there, at least in memory. It will resurface during moments of fatigue, doubt, or longing. That doesn't mean you should return to it. It means you are human. Progress does not require erasing who you were. It requires deciding, again and again, who you are becoming.

And each time you choose to continue—quietly, imperfectly—you weaken the pull. Not because the old life disappears, but because the new one gains weight. Eventually, the balance shifts. What once felt like gravity becomes history.

Chapter 22

Starting is a Practice, Not a One-Time Event

One of the most persistent misunderstandings about starting is the belief that it happens once. That there is a beginning you cross, a threshold you pass, and from that point on, momentum carries you forward without interruption. This belief is comforting—and incomplete. Starting is not a moment you conquer; it is a practice you return to. Again and again. In different forms. At different stages. Often when you least want to.

The idea that starting should be a single decisive act creates unnecessary pressure. It frames the beginning as something you must get right, something you either succeed at or fail. When people inevitably encounter friction later—hesitation, doubt, fatigue—they assume they've lost their way. In reality, they've simply reached another beginning. Growth is not linear; it is cyclical. Each new level of expansion asks you to start again, often from a place that feels strangely familiar.

This is why starting feels uncomfortable even after you've already begun. You don't just start once—you start at every new edge. A new responsibility. A deeper commitment. A bolder expression of who you are becoming. Each time, the nervous system reacts as if it's the first. The discomfort does not mean you're regressing. It means the practice is continuing.

Viewing starting as a practice reframes resistance entirely. Resistance is no longer evidence that something is wrong; it is part of the rhythm. Just as physical training involves repeated stress and recovery, psychological growth involves repeated entry into uncertainty. You step forward. You stabilize. You rest. Then you step forward again. The mistake is expecting the practice to end.

When starting is treated as a one-time event, people chase permanence. They want to reach a place where effort disappears and confidence becomes automatic. While some behaviors do become easier over time, growth itself never becomes static. Life continues to present new thresholds. New seasons require new starts. The person you become must keep initiating, not because something is broken, but because life is alive.

This perspective also changes how you respond to pauses. If starting is a single event, stopping feels like failure. If starting is a practice, stopping becomes part of the cycle. Rest does not erase progress. Pauses do not invalidate momentum. What matters is the ability to return. The practice is not uninterrupted motion—it is repeated re-engagement.

Another important shift occurs when you stop idolizing the first step. The first step matters, but it is not more important than the second, the fifth, or the fiftieth. Each requires a willingness to begin again. Each asks you to override hesitation, not because you lack discipline, but because starting is simply what this season requires. The skill is not bravery—it is familiarity with beginning.

Over time, this familiarity builds resilience. You stop treating new beginnings as emergencies. You don't dramatize hesitation or panic when clarity fades. You recognize the signals. *This is a new edge. This is where starting lives.* That recognition alone reduces friction. You're no longer surprised by the discomfort. You expect it.

This is where many people quietly level up. They stop seeing themselves as someone who "once started" and begin seeing themselves as someone who knows how to start. That distinction is profound. It means you no longer fear future uncertainty as much, because you trust your ability to re-enter the process. You don't need to have everything figured out— you know how to take the next honest step.

Starting as a practice also restores agency. Instead of waiting for the perfect moment, you create momentum through repetition. You don't need inspiration to strike. You don't need permission. You don't need guarantees. You rely on something sturdier: the knowledge that you can begin, even when conditions are imperfect. Especially when they are.

There is humility in this approach. It accepts that you will not outgrow uncertainty. That you will not arrive at a final version of yourself who never doubts or hesitates. But there is also empowerment in it. Because you stop measuring yourself by how confident you feel and start measuring yourself by how willing you are to engage.

This chapter matters because it dismantles the illusion of arrival. There is no place where starting becomes unnecessary. There is only deeper participation. Each chapter of your life will ask you to begin again—in relationships, work, creativity, and self-understanding. The people who build meaningful lives are not those who start once and coast. They are those who keep returning to the practice, without resentment, without drama, and without self-betrayal.

Starting is not a rite of passage you graduate from. It is a skill you refine. A muscle you use. A rhythm you learn to trust. And once you understand that, the fear of beginning loses much of its power. Because you're no longer asking yourself to do something extraordinary. You're simply doing what you already know how to do.

You start again.

Chapter 23

The Day You Realize
You're No Longer Waiting

The realization doesn't arrive with celebration. There is no clear before-and-after moment, no dramatic line in the sand where you declare that waiting is over. In fact, when it happens, you may not recognize it at all. The day you stop waiting feels remarkably ordinary. You wake up, move through your routines, and do what needs to be done. The difference is not in what the day looks like—it's in how you inhabit it.

For a long time, waiting shaped everything. You waited for clarity before acting, for confidence before committing, for permission before choosing. Even when you were busy, there was a sense that life was on hold, that something real would begin later. Waiting became a posture, a way of relating to the future. You were always preparing, always considering, always just short of beginning. And because waiting was familiar, it felt almost invisible.

Then, slowly, something shifted.

You didn't stop feeling uncertainty. You didn't suddenly know where everything was going. What changed was your relationship to those feelings. You no longer paused your life until doubt resolved itself. You acted alongside it. You made decisions without requiring emotional certainty. You stopped rehearsing your future and started participating in it. The waiting didn't end because conditions changed—it ended because you did.

The first sign is subtle: you catch yourself responding instead of hesitating. An opportunity appears and you engage rather than overanalyze. A problem arises and you address it rather than delay. You don't feel braver—you feel present. The gap between intention and action narrows. You don't need to psych yourself up. You don't need to talk yourself into motion. You simply move.

Another sign is how time feels. Waiting stretches time. It makes days feel repetitive and years feel blurred. When you stop waiting, time gains texture. Moments carry weight. Progress may still be slow, but it feels directional. You're no longer measuring life by how long you've been thinking— you're measuring it by what you've been doing. Even small actions feel anchored because they're part of a lived sequence, not a postponed plan.

You also notice a shift in your internal dialogue. The constant questioning softens. You stop asking, *Should I start?* and start asking, *What's next?* The energy once spent debating is now spent adjusting. You're no longer trying to decide whether you're allowed to move—you're deciding how to move better. This is a quiet but profound change. It marks the difference between contemplation and participation.

Waiting has a way of making you feel separate from your own life, like an observer standing just outside the action. When you stop waiting, you step back in. You feel the friction, the effort, the uncertainty—but you also feel agency. You're not imagining outcomes anymore; you're influencing them. Even when things don't go as planned, there is a sense of ownership. *This is happening because I'm here, not because I stayed back.*

One of the most surprising aspects of this shift is how little drama it contains. You may have expected a surge of confidence or clarity. Instead, you find steadiness. You trust your ability to adapt more than your ability to predict. You don't need everything to make sense in advance. You've learned that understanding comes through engagement, not anticipation.

Relationships change subtly as well. You stop explaining yourself as much. You don't seek validation for every choice. You're less reactive to other people's opinions because you're no longer using them to decide whether to act. This doesn't make you distant or detached—it makes you grounded. You listen, you consider, but you no longer pause your life waiting for agreement.

The day you realize you're no longer waiting is also the day self-trust becomes tangible. Not as a belief, but as a pattern. You've seen yourself begin again and again. You've watched yourself continue through uncertainty. You've learned that hesitation doesn't have to stop you. That knowledge changes how you face the future. New challenges still bring discomfort, but they don't bring paralysis.

It's important to understand that waiting doesn't vanish completely. It still whispers occasionally, especially in moments of fatigue or doubt. The difference is that it no longer defines you. You recognize it for what it is—a habit you once relied on. And habits, once seen clearly, lose their authority.

This chapter is not about arrival. It's about orientation. You haven't reached a final destination. You haven't solved life. What you've done is step out of the holding pattern. You're no longer circling the runway, burning fuel, waiting for permission to land. You're on the ground now, moving, navigating, adjusting course as needed.

The day you realize you're no longer waiting may never stand out on a calendar. But it will change how every future day unfolds. Because once waiting stops being your default, life stops feeling like something that's about to begin.

It begins because you're already in it.

Chapter 24

What Starting Ultimately Gives You

People often believe that starting is a means to an end. That its value lies in what it produces—success, freedom, fulfillment, a different life on the other side. And while starting can lead to all of those outcomes, none of them capture its deepest gift. What starting ultimately gives you is not a result. It gives you a *relationship*—with yourself, with time, and with life as it actually unfolds.

The first thing starting gives you is **agency**. Not the abstract idea of control, but the lived experience of influence. When you start, you move out of reaction and into participation. Life stops feeling like something that happens to you and begins to feel like something you engage with. Even when circumstances are difficult, even when outcomes are uncertain, there is a grounding sense that you are not merely enduring—you are choosing. That shift alone changes how you experience everything else.

Starting also gives you **honesty**. Waiting allows you to hide behind intention. You can tell yourself who you are going to be, what you're capable of, what you'll do someday. Starting removes that buffer. It puts you in contact with reality—your energy, your limits, your strengths, your preferences. This honesty is not always comfortable, but it is clarifying. You stop living in imagined versions of yourself and begin relating to who you actually are. And from that place, real growth becomes possible.

Another gift of starting is **self-trust**. Not the kind that comes from affirmations or reassurance, but the kind that comes from evidence. Each time you begin without guarantees and continue anyway, you teach yourself something important: *I can handle this*. You learn that fear does not mean danger, that uncertainty does not mean collapse, that imperfection does not mean failure. This trust accumulates quietly. Over time, it becomes a steady internal reference point—one that does not depend on external validation or perfect conditions.

Starting also changes your relationship with **time**. When you're waiting, time feels like an enemy. It slips away while you prepare, consider, and postpone. When you start, time becomes an ally. Even slow progress feels meaningful because it's directional. You stop measuring life by how long you've been thinking and start measuring it by how present you've been. Days carry more weight. Years feel less abstract. You're no longer trying to outrun time—you're using it.

There is also a deep sense of **aliveness** that starting restores. Not excitement, necessarily, but engagement. You feel more awake to your own life. Challenges feel sharper. Successes feel earned. Even setbacks feel instructive rather than numbing. Starting reconnects you to the texture of experience. It pulls you out of autopilot and back into relationship with what you're building and becoming.

One of the quieter rewards of starting is **freedom from regret**. Not because everything works out, but because you know you participated. You tried. You learned. You adjusted. Regret thrives in the space between desire and inaction. Starting collapses that space. Even when outcomes fall short, the question changes from *What if?* to *What did this teach me?* That shift matters more than success itself.

Starting also reshapes how you relate to **failure**. When you haven't started, failure feels catastrophic because it threatens the fantasy of who you might have been. When you have started, failure becomes contextual. It's no longer a verdict on your worth—it's feedback within a process you're already part of. This reframing reduces fear and increases resilience. You stop protecting yourself from failure and start using it.

There is a relational gift as well. When you start, you show up differently with others. You listen more honestly. You speak with more clarity. You stop seeking permission and start sharing perspective. This doesn't make you rigid or self-centered—it makes you authentic. Relationships deepen when you're no longer hiding parts of yourself behind postponement. Some connections may shift. Others will strengthen. All will become more real.

Perhaps the most meaningful gift of starting is **alignment**. Not perfection, not constant ease, but coherence. Your actions begin to match your values. Your days reflect what matters to you. Even when life is demanding, there is less internal conflict. You're no longer divided between who you are and who you wish you were. That alignment creates a sense of peace that comfort alone can never provide.

This chapter matters because many people believe starting is only worthwhile if it leads to a specific outcome. But starting is valuable even when outcomes change, evolve, or fall apart. Its real value lies in what it restores: agency, honesty, self-trust, aliveness, and alignment. These are not things you earn at the end of a journey. They are things you cultivate by participating in it.

Starting does not guarantee happiness. It guarantees *engagement.* And engagement is what makes a life feel lived rather than endured. It is what turns time into experience and intention into reality.

You don't start to arrive somewhere perfect. You start to come back to yourself.

Chapter 25

The Legacy of Those Who Begin

Legacy is often misunderstood. People imagine it as something grand and distant—buildings named after you, achievements etched into history, accomplishments that outlive your physical presence. This version of legacy is seductive because it feels impressive, but it's also misleading. Most legacies are not built through spectacle. They are built through patterns. Through the way a person chooses to engage with their life, day after day, especially when no one is watching.

The true legacy of those who begin is not what they accomplish—it is what they make possible.

When you start, you give others permission without ever saying a word. Your movement disrupts the quiet agreement that says *this is just how things are*. It introduces a new data point into the world: someone chose to act. Someone chose to step forward despite uncertainty. Someone chose not to wait. That example matters more than advice ever could, because it is embodied. It shows what is possible rather than explaining it.

This is why starting has a ripple effect you may never fully see. The courage you practice privately becomes visible in ways you can't control. People notice shifts in how you speak, how you decide, how you tolerate discomfort. They sense that you are less reactive, less resigned, more engaged. Even if they don't know what you're building, they feel that something has changed. And that feeling stays with them.

Legacy also lives in the conversations that change because you started. When you speak from experience rather than theory, your words carry weight. You don't persuade—you resonate. You don't preach—you reflect. People trust what you say not because you're confident, but because you've lived what you're describing. That credibility is earned, not claimed.

Another quiet form of legacy shows up in the way you relate to fear. When you stop treating fear as a stop sign and start treating it as information, you model a different relationship with uncertainty. Those around you learn—consciously or not—that fear does not have to dictate decisions. That discomfort is survivable. That growth does not require recklessness, only willingness. This reframing can alter how others approach their own edges.

For parents, leaders, partners, and mentors, this legacy is especially powerful. Children rarely follow instructions as closely as they follow examples. Teams rarely adopt values that aren't demonstrated. When you begin—even imperfectly— you normalize effort, adaptability, and courage. You show that growth is not reserved for a certain age, status, or personality type. It is something available to anyone willing to engage.

There is also a deeply personal legacy that unfolds within you. Each time you start, you rewrite your own internal history. You stop seeing your life as a series of missed chances and begin seeing it as a sequence of responses. You shift from regret to participation. That internal legacy shapes how you face future challenges. You carry forward the knowledge that you are not someone who waits indefinitely—you are someone who begins again.

Legacy is not only about what remains after you're gone. It's about what remains *within you* as time passes. Starting leaves behind a residue of self-respect. Even when outcomes are uncertain, even when paths change, you know you honored something important. You didn't abandon yourself. That knowledge alters how you age, how you reflect, how you relate to the story of your own life.

It's also important to understand that legacy does not require consistency at all costs. Those who begin are not those who never falter. They are those who return. Who restart. Who refuse to let hesitation become identity. The legacy is not perfection—it's persistence without self-betrayal.

Most people underestimate the cumulative impact of choosing to start. One decision rarely changes the world. But a pattern does. A pattern of beginning reshapes families, organizations, and cultures over time. It challenges stagnation not through rebellion, but through example. It quietly raises the standard for what it means to be alive rather than merely functional.

This chapter matters because many people believe their actions only matter if they lead to visible success. In truth, your willingness to begin matters regardless of outcome. It alters the environment you move through. It influences the people who share space with you. It changes the internal narrative you pass down—to others and to yourself.

The legacy of those who begin is not loud. It is durable. It does not rely on recognition. It lives in the expanded sense of possibility left in its wake.

You may never fully see the impact of your starting. But it will be there—in the lives you touch, the conversations you shift, and the future selves you make possible.

And that, quietly and unmistakably, is how real legacy is built.

Chapter 26

The Courage to Be Seen Before You're Ready

There is a particular kind of fear that emerges only after you've begun. It is not the fear of failure or the fear of uncertainty—you've already learned how to move alongside those. This fear is more intimate, more personal. It is the fear of being seen while you are still becoming. Seen without polish. Seen without certainty. Seen before the story makes sense. For many people, this fear is more paralyzing than the fear of starting itself.

When you were waiting, invisibility was a form of protection. You could dream privately, imagine quietly, and keep your uncertainty hidden. Starting changed that. Even small actions create traces. Someone notices. A question is asked. A shift is observed. You are no longer entirely anonymous in your intention. And with that visibility comes vulnerability.

The discomfort of being seen before you're ready often shows up as hesitation around sharing, committing publicly, or fully owning what you're doing. You might downplay your efforts, speak about them vaguely, or avoid talking about them altogether. This isn't dishonesty—it's self-preservation. You are protecting something fragile. A version of yourself that is still forming.

What makes this stage difficult is that visibility feels premature. You don't yet have results to point to. You don't yet feel grounded in a new identity. You may worry that being seen too early invites judgment, criticism, or misunderstanding. And those fears are not unfounded. When you step into visibility before you feel established, you open yourself to opinions you didn't ask for and standards you didn't set.

But invisibility has a cost.

Remaining unseen for too long can quietly stall progress. You stay half-committed, half-expressed. You keep one foot in the old identity while testing the new one in isolation. This limbo feels safe, but it limits growth. Certain opportunities, feedback, and connections only appear when you allow yourself to be visible—when you let the world respond to who you are becoming, not just who you were.

The courage required here is not performative confidence. It is not about announcing yourself loudly or pretending you have it all figured out. It is the courage to say, *This is what I'm working on*, without needing approval or validation. It is the willingness to let your work, your effort, and your evolution be imperfectly observed.

Being seen before you're ready forces honesty. You can no longer hide behind preparation. You can no longer adjust the story endlessly in your head. Reality enters the picture. People react. Some encourage. Some misunderstand. Some project their own fears onto you. This feedback is not always pleasant—but it is clarifying. It teaches you where you are grounded and where you are still seeking permission.

There is also a subtle identity shift that happens when you allow yourself to be seen. You begin to relate to your actions differently. They feel more real. More consequential. Visibility creates accountability—not the harsh kind, but the grounding kind. You're no longer starting in theory. You're starting in the world. That matters.

This stage often brings up old patterns around approval. You may notice how sensitive you feel to other people's reactions. Praise may feel relieving. Indifference may sting. Criticism may feel personal. These reactions are not signs that you shouldn't be visible—they are signs that identity is still forming. Over time, as your sense of self stabilizes, visibility becomes less charged. You stop needing every response to confirm your worth.

The mistake many people make is waiting until they feel confident enough to be seen. But confidence does not precede visibility—it follows it. Confidence is built by surviving exposure. By realizing that misunderstanding is tolerable. That criticism is not fatal. That being seen does not strip you of agency. Each time you allow yourself to be visible and continue anyway, something strengthens internally.

This chapter is not an invitation to overshare or rush into exposure. It's an invitation to notice where invisibility has become another form of waiting. To recognize when privacy is protective versus when it is limiting. To understand that some aspects of growth require witness—not for validation, but for integration.

Being seen before you're ready does not mean being reckless with your vulnerability. It means being honest about where you are. It means allowing your evolution to exist outside your own head. It means trusting that you do not need to arrive before you're allowed to participate.

The courage to be seen is not about confidence. It's about self-respect. It's about refusing to hide simply because you're still learning. And when you choose that courage—even in small ways—you step into a deeper form of starting. One that no longer depends on invisibility to feel safe.

You don't need to be finished to be seen. You only need to be willing to continue.

Chapter 27

Choosing Yourself Without Burning Everything Down

One of the most persistent myths about choosing yourself is that it requires destruction. Burning bridges. Quitting dramatically. Cutting people off. Walking away from everything that came before. This myth is seductive because it frames self-commitment as bold and uncompromising. But it is also deeply misleading. In reality, most meaningful acts of self-choice are quiet, incremental, and almost invisible from the outside. Choosing yourself does not require setting your life on fire—it requires setting a direction and honoring it consistently.

The fear that choosing yourself will harm others is real. Many people have built their identities around being dependable, accommodating, and needed. They have learned—often early—that their value comes from being available, agreeable, and low-maintenance. When they consider prioritizing their own growth, guilt surfaces immediately. *Isn't this selfish? What about everyone else?* This guilt keeps them frozen, mistaking self-erasure for responsibility.

But choosing yourself is not the same as abandoning others. It is the difference between neglect and neglecting *yourself*. When you consistently ignore your own needs, desires, and direction, the cost shows up eventually—often as resentment, exhaustion, or quiet disengagement. Those outcomes harm relationships far more than honest boundaries ever could. Choosing yourself, done thoughtfully, actually preserves connection by preventing the slow decay that comes from living out of alignment.

What makes this choice difficult is that it often requires disappointing people—not because you're doing something wrong, but because you're doing something different. Others may have grown comfortable with who you were when you were easier to predict, easier to rely on, easier to access. When you begin to choose yourself, even in small ways, that predictability changes. Some people will adjust. Others will resist. Their discomfort is not a verdict on your decision—it is a response to change.

Choosing yourself without burning everything down means learning how to **integrate** rather than replace. You don't discard your responsibilities; you renegotiate how you carry them. You don't reject relationships; you bring more honesty into them. You don't escape your life; you reshape your role within it. This approach requires patience, because integration is slower than escape. But it is also far more sustainable.

Another challenge is internal. When you begin choosing yourself, you may feel unfamiliar to yourself. You're no longer operating solely from obligation or expectation. You're listening inward. This can feel destabilizing at first. You may question whether you're being unreasonable or dramatic. This is not intuition failing—it's identity adjusting. You are learning how to include yourself in your own decisions.

Choosing yourself also involves boundaries, and boundaries often get misunderstood as ultimatums. In reality, boundaries are clarifications. They communicate what you can and cannot sustain. They are not punishments; they are information. When you set boundaries without aggression or apology, you create space for relationships to evolve rather than implode. Some will meet you there. Some won't. Both outcomes are informative.

There is also a subtle courage required to choose yourself when the results are not immediate. You may not see dramatic improvements right away. You may still feel tired. You may still feel uncertain. The difference is that your effort is now aligned with your direction. You are no longer expending energy maintaining a life that doesn't fit. That alignment, even when imperfect, reduces internal conflict. And reduced conflict creates capacity.

This chapter matters because many people delay starting out of fear that self-choice requires total upheaval. They wait for a moment when walking away feels justified. That moment rarely comes. Change doesn't need justification—it needs intention. Choosing yourself is not a one-time declaration. It is a series of small, consistent decisions that signal to yourself and others that your life includes you.

The paradox is this: when you choose yourself thoughtfully, you often become more present, not less. More honest. More engaged. More capable of showing up without resentment. The relationships and responsibilities that remain become clearer, cleaner, and more sustainable. What falls away does so because it no longer fits—not because you destroyed it.

You don't have to burn your life down to build something meaningful. You only have to stop disappearing inside it.

Choosing yourself is not an act of rebellion.

It is an act of return.

Chapter 28

The Moment You Stop Negotiating With Fear

For a long time, fear has had a seat at the table. Not as an enemy, but as a negotiator. It hasn't shouted or threatened—it's been reasonable. It's asked for more time, more proof, more reassurance. It's suggested compromises. *Start later. Start smaller. Wait until things feel more stable.* And because fear has spoken calmly, intelligently, you've listened. You've engaged. You've negotiated.

What changes is not that fear disappears.

What changes is that you stop negotiating with it.

This moment does not arrive with confidence. It arrives with clarity. A quiet, steady knowing that fear has already said everything it has to say—and nothing new is coming. You realize you've heard these arguments before. You recognize the loop. The same concerns, the same doubts, the same warnings, recycled with different details but the same conclusion: *Don't move yet.*

This is not the moment fear is defeated. It is the moment fear is no longer promoted to decision-maker.

Negotiating with fear feels responsible because it sounds like prudence. You weigh risks. You imagine scenarios. You try to outthink uncertainty. But what you eventually notice is that the negotiation never ends. Fear does not reach a point of satisfaction. It does not say, *Okay, now you're ready.* Its job is not to approve movement—it is to minimize exposure. As long as you keep negotiating, fear keeps winning by default.

The shift happens when you recognize that fear is not asking for answers—it's asking for control.

Once you see this, something inside you settles. Not because the path is suddenly safe, but because the conversation changes. You stop trying to convince fear. You stop explaining your reasons. You stop promising to revisit the decision later. You acknowledge the fear—and proceed anyway. This is not recklessness. It is boundaries.

Stopping negotiation does not mean ignoring fear. It means listening without obeying. Fear becomes information, not instruction. You take note of its concerns, adjust where necessary, and move forward without waiting for emotional permission. This distinction is subtle but profound. It marks the difference between being led by fear and being informed by it.

At first, this feels uncomfortable. Negotiation gave you the illusion of safety. It made hesitation feel productive. Letting go of that process can feel exposed, even irresponsible. But over time, something steadier replaces it: resolve. Not urgency. Not pressure. Resolve is quiet. It doesn't argue. It simply continues.

You may notice that fear gets louder briefly when negotiation ends. This is normal. When fear loses influence, it escalates. It tries new angles. It brings up worst-case scenarios. It questions your judgment. This surge is not a sign you're wrong—it's a sign the pattern has been disrupted. Fear is adjusting to a new role.

What's different now is that you don't pause to engage. You don't reopen the debate. You keep moving. And in doing so, you teach your nervous system something essential: fear can be present without being in charge. This lesson cannot be learned through reasoning alone. It must be embodied.

Over time, the internal dynamic changes. Fear doesn't vanish, but it stops dominating your attention. You stop organizing your life around avoiding discomfort. You stop treating safety as the highest value. You begin valuing alignment, honesty, and participation more. This reordering of values changes how decisions feel. You no longer ask, *How do I make this feel safe?* You ask, *How do I make this true?*

This chapter matters because many people believe fear must be resolved before action is possible. In reality, fear is rarely resolved through thought. It is resolved through repetition. Through doing the thing and surviving it. Through discovering that discomfort does not equal danger. The moment you stop negotiating is the moment that learning accelerates.

You don't become fearless. You become decisive.

Decisive does not mean rigid. It means you stop outsourcing authority to a feeling that was never meant to lead your life. You reclaim authorship. You accept responsibility—not just for outcomes, but for direction. That acceptance brings a strange kind of peace. The peace of no longer debating your own existence.

Fear may still walk beside you. That's fine.
It just doesn't get a vote anymore.

And when fear loses its vote, starting stops being a question.

It becomes a way of living.

Chapter 29
Living Without the Backup Plan

There comes a point, often unnoticed at first, when the backup plan quietly loses its grip. You didn't announce it. You didn't ceremoniously abandon it. It simply stopped being the place your mind retreats to when things feel uncertain. For a long time, the backup plan served a purpose. It was a psychological escape hatch—a way to soothe fear by reminding yourself that if this didn't work, you could always go back, pivot safely, or return to something familiar. The backup plan felt responsible. It felt mature. It felt smart.

But it also kept one foot planted in the old life.

Living with a backup plan subtly divides your energy. Even when you're taking action, part of you is watching for signs that it's time to retreat. You move forward, but cautiously. You test rather than commit. You keep evaluating whether this path deserves your full presence. This split attention is not laziness—it's self-protection. But protection has a cost. It prevents full engagement, and without full engagement, depth is impossible.

This chapter is not about recklessness. It's about honesty.

A backup plan becomes limiting when it's no longer a contingency and starts becoming an identity anchor. When you tell yourself, *I'll try this, but I can always go back*, you never fully arrive. You don't let the new life demand adaptation. You don't let challenges reshape you. You remain psychologically loyal to the old version of yourself, even as you experiment with becoming someone new.

The moment the backup plan loosens is the moment you stop treating your current path as provisional. Not because success is guaranteed, but because retreat is no longer the organizing principle. You stop asking, *Is this worth continuing?* every time things get hard. You start asking, *What needs to change so this can work?* That shift—from evaluation to engagement—is subtle, but decisive.

Living without the backup plan does not mean you ignore reality. It means you stop using escape as emotional regulation. You face difficulty without immediately imagining an exit. You allow discomfort to exist without translating it into a reason to quit. This builds a different kind of strength—the strength that comes from staying long enough to adapt.

For many people, the backup plan is not external. It's internal. It's the identity they can fall back on. *I'm really a practical person. This was just an experiment. I never expected much anyway.* These narratives soften the blow of uncertainty, but they also soften commitment. When things don't work immediately, the backup identity steps in to protect you from disappointment—at the cost of growth.

Letting go of the backup plan often brings up fear, not because the path becomes more dangerous, but because it becomes more real. Without a psychological escape, effort matters more. Choices carry more weight. You can no longer hide behind the idea that this was temporary. This can feel heavy—but it is also clarifying. You begin to take yourself seriously.

There is also grief here. The backup plan represents safety, familiarity, and a version of yourself that knew how to survive. Releasing it does not mean that version was wrong. It means it no longer needs to lead. Acknowledging that loss—without rushing past it—is part of maturing into a new way of living.

What most people discover is that when the backup plan fades, presence increases. You listen more closely. You respond more thoughtfully. You become more creative, not because pressure increased, but because avoidance decreased. You stop conserving energy for retreat and start investing it in refinement. This is when real skill develops. This is when momentum deepens.

Importantly, living without a backup plan does not mean you trap yourself. It means you stop fantasizing about escape while pretending to commit. If a path truly no longer fits, you will know—not because it's uncomfortable, but because it no longer aligns. That decision will come from clarity, not fear. The difference is everything.

This chapter matters because many people believe they are committed when they are still hedging. They wonder why progress feels shallow, why confidence hasn't fully formed, why doubt keeps returning. Often, it's because part of them is still holding the door open to the past. Growth requires some doors to close—not dramatically, but definitively.

When the backup plan loses its power, you don't feel reckless. You feel grounded. You stop scanning for exits and start building interiors. You stop rehearsing what you'll do if this fails and start learning how to make it work.

Living without the backup plan does not guarantee success. It guarantees presence.

And presence is what turns starting into a life—not an experiment.

Chapter 30

Becoming Someone Who Trusts Their Own Direction

There is a subtle but profound shift that happens near the end of this journey—not the end of the work, but the end of a certain internal dependence. You stop looking outward so often. You stop searching for confirmation, reassurance, or signs that you're on the "right" path. Not because you've become stubborn or closed off, but because something steadier has taken root. You begin to trust your own direction.

This trust does not arrive as certainty. It arrives as orientation.

For much of your life, direction may have come from external structures—education, career ladders, cultural expectations, other people's opinions about what made sense. Even when you rebelled against those structures, they still defined the edges of your choices. You reacted to them. You measured yourself against them. Trusting your own direction requires something different. It requires learning how to navigate without constantly checking whether you're approved, validated, or understood.

This is uncomfortable at first. External reference points are efficient. They reduce ambiguity. They tell you how you're doing. When you begin trusting your own direction, that feedback becomes quieter. You don't get instant signals. You don't always know how it looks from the outside. You must rely on something more internal—how aligned an action feels, how honest a choice is, how consistently you're willing to show up.

Trusting your direction doesn't mean you stop listening to others. It means you stop outsourcing the final decision. Advice becomes input, not instruction. You can hear multiple perspectives without losing your center. You can disagree without defensiveness. You can change course without collapsing into self-doubt. This flexibility is a sign of trust, not weakness.

Another marker of this shift is how you relate to comparison. When you don't trust your direction, other people's progress feels like a referendum on your own. You constantly recalibrate—*Am I behind? Am I ahead? Am I doing this right?* When you trust your direction, comparison loses urgency. Other people's paths become interesting rather than threatening. You can learn from them without needing to imitate them.

There is also a change in how you experience mistakes. When direction comes from outside, mistakes feel like violations. You've broken a rule. You've failed a test. When direction comes from within, mistakes feel like navigation errors—information that helps you adjust. They don't define you. They guide you. This reframing reduces fear and increases experimentation. You're more willing to try, because being wrong no longer threatens your sense of self.

Trusting your own direction also brings a new relationship with patience. You stop rushing outcomes to prove legitimacy. You understand that alignment compounds over time. You're less tempted by shortcuts that promise speed at the cost of coherence. You choose depth over display. This patience is not passive—it's intentional. It's grounded in the knowledge that meaningful things take time to integrate.

This chapter matters because many people confuse self-trust with self-confidence. Confidence is emotional. It rises and falls. Trust is behavioral. It's built through repetition. Every time you choose based on alignment rather than approval, trust strengthens. Every time you stay present through uncertainty instead of escaping into consensus, trust deepens. Over time, these moments accumulate into a way of being.

You may still feel doubt. You may still feel fear. Trusting your direction does not eliminate these experiences. It changes how much authority they have. Doubt becomes a question, not a verdict. Fear becomes a signal, not a stop sign. You no longer wait for them to disappear before you move. You move while carrying them.

One of the quietest indicators of this shift is how you speak about your life. There is less explanation, less justification. You don't need to narrate every choice or defend every pivot. You're not hiding—you're settled. The story is still unfolding, and you're comfortable letting it unfold in real time.

By the time you reach this point, starting is no longer something you do occasionally. It's embedded in how you live. You don't wait for certainty. You don't negotiate endlessly. You don't require permission. You orient, you act, you adjust. Over and over. This rhythm becomes familiar. Trust grows not because everything works out, but because you know how to respond when it doesn't.

Becoming someone who trusts their own direction is not about having answers. It's about having a relationship with uncertainty that doesn't paralyze you. It's about choosing alignment over applause. Engagement over explanation. Presence over prediction.

You don't need to know exactly where you're going. You need to trust how you move.

And once you trust that, starting is no longer something you fear.

It's simply how you live.

Chapter 31

The Life That Could Only Exist Because You Started

There is a version of your life that cannot be planned in advance. It cannot be visualized clearly, reverse-engineered, or predicted with any accuracy. It does not respond to vision boards or five-year plans. It only reveals itself through movement. This life—the one that feels real, textured, and deeply yours—could only exist because you started.

Before you began, this life was invisible. Not absent, just unreachable. It lived beyond the edge of hesitation, beyond the place where thinking alone could take you. You may have sensed it in fleeting moments—a pull, a restlessness, a quiet knowing—but you couldn't access it without crossing a threshold. Starting was the act that made contact possible.

What's striking about this life is how different it looks from what you imagined. Not necessarily better in every way, not free from struggle or uncertainty—but truer. More dimensional. Less theoretical. You don't live inside constant anticipation anymore. You live inside response. Things happen, and you meet them. You are no longer rehearsing a future self—you are inhabiting a present one.

This life has edges. It has friction. It asks things of you. But it also gives things back that waiting never could. It gives you texture—days that feel distinct instead of blurred. It gives you stories that are lived rather than imagined. It gives you a sense of authorship, even when the plot twists in ways you didn't expect.

One of the quiet changes is how you relate to possibility. Before, possibility felt abstract and overwhelming. Too many options, too many risks, too much uncertainty. Now, possibility feels grounded. You don't need to hold every door open. You move through one at a time. You discover what fits by living it. Possibility becomes experiential rather than hypothetical.

This life also brings humility. Starting dismantles the fantasy of control. You learn quickly that effort does not guarantee outcomes, and that unpredictability is not a flaw in the system—it *is* the system. But instead of making you cynical, this humility makes you resilient. You stop demanding perfection from the process. You adapt. You respond. You continue.

There is also a deeper kind of gratitude that emerges—not the performative kind, but the grounded kind. You appreciate what you have not because it is ideal, but because it is earned through participation. Even the hard parts carry meaning, because they are connected to choices you made rather than circumstances you avoided. This gratitude is quiet, but it is steady.

The life that emerges after starting is not one where fear disappears. Fear still visits. Doubt still speaks. Uncertainty still exists. The difference is that these experiences no longer define the boundaries of your movement. They are part of the landscape, not the gatekeepers. You don't need to conquer them. You move with them.

You may also notice that this life feels less performative. You're not trying to prove as much—to yourself or to others. The metrics that once mattered lose their grip. You care less about how it looks and more about how it feels to live it. Alignment becomes more important than optics. Substance more important than speed.

This chapter matters because many people believe starting is about changing outcomes. In truth, starting changes *experience*. It alters how you inhabit time, how you relate to challenge, how you measure a life. The rewards are not always visible, but they are deeply felt. You don't just get a different future—you get a different present.

And perhaps the most important realization is this: this life did not appear because you were brave enough, smart enough, or prepared enough. It appeared because you were willing to move without guarantees. Because you accepted that meaning is not found by waiting for clarity, but by engaging with uncertainty.

The life you are living now—imperfect, evolving, unfinished—is not a consolation prize. It is the direct result of choosing participation over postponement. It is a life that could not have been accessed through thinking alone.

You didn't arrive here because everything worked out.

You arrived here because you started.

And because you did, this life—your life—finally had somewhere to begin.

Chapter 32

The Day You Stop Asking "What If" and Start Saying "This Is"

For a long time, your inner world was dominated by a question. *What if?*

What if you fail.

What if you succeed.

What if you're wrong.

What if it's too late.

What if you're not enough.

The question felt intelligent. Responsible. Necessary. It gave you something to do instead of acting. It kept your mind busy while your life stayed still. *What if* became a way of living just ahead of yourself—always preparing for a future that never quite arrived.

Then, slowly, without ceremony, the question lost its grip.

Not because you found all the answers—but because the answers stopped mattering as much as the experience. You stopped living in hypothetical futures and started inhabiting the present one. The language inside you changed. Not loudly. Not dramatically. Just enough to notice.

This is.

This is where I am.

This is what I'm building.

This is what today requires.

This is imperfect, unfinished, and real.

The shift from *what if* to *this is* is one of the most stabilizing transitions a person can make. *What if* keeps you suspended between possibilities. *This is* grounds you in reality. It doesn't eliminate uncertainty—it contextualizes it. You're no longer trying to predict the entire path. You're responding to what's actually happening.

Before, *what if* made fear feel endless. There was always another scenario to consider, another outcome to brace for. Now, fear has limits. It belongs to specific moments, not your entire future. You deal with it as it appears, instead of carrying it everywhere in advance. This alone frees an enormous amount of energy.

Saying *this is* does not mean resignation. It means clarity. It means you stop arguing with reality and start working with it. You see what's in front of you without dramatizing it or minimizing it. You no longer need the situation to be different before you engage. Engagement becomes the way things change.

This is also the moment when self-deception becomes harder. When you lived in *what if*, you could imagine progress without making it. You could feel close to change without committing to it. *This is* removes that buffer. It asks for honesty. Not harsh honesty—grounded honesty. The kind that allows you to say, *This part is working. This part isn't. This is where I am today.* And from that honesty comes power.

Power not in the sense of control, but in the sense of response. You stop reacting to imagined futures and start responding to real conditions. You make decisions based on evidence, not anxiety. You adjust based on experience, not fear. This is how people stop spinning and start stabilizing.

Another subtle shift happens here: you stop narrating your life as much. When you were stuck in *what if*, everything needed explanation. You justified delays. You explained intentions. You defended your pace. When you live in *this is*, explanation loses urgency. You don't need to convince anyone—often not even yourself. The work speaks. The movement speaks.

This chapter matters because many people believe their anxiety comes from uncertainty, when in reality it comes from living in imagined futures instead of present realities. The mind was never meant to inhabit endless hypotheticals. It was meant to respond to what is. Starting brings you back into that relationship with life.

You may still think about the future. You may still plan. But planning no longer replaces living. It supports it. The future becomes something you're building into, not bracing for.

This is does not mean everything is resolved. It means everything is happening. It means you've stopped asking whether you're allowed to be here. It means you've stopped waiting for your life to begin. It means you've accepted that this moment—this imperfect, active, evolving moment—is the only place anything real can happen.

And once you're living from *this is* instead of *what if*, something quiet but profound settles in.

You're no longer haunted by the life you didn't live.

You're too busy living the one that exists because you started.

Chapter 33

You Were Never Behind

There is a belief that quietly poisons more lives than failure ever could: the belief that you are late. That you missed your window. That if you were going to start, you would have done it by now. This belief doesn't shout—it sighs. It settles into the background of your thinking and reframes everything you consider. *What's the point now? Others are so far ahead. I should have known sooner.* And with that belief in place, starting feels less like possibility and more like embarrassment.

But here is the truth most people never hear, and almost no one internalizes until much later: **you were never behind.**

You were becoming.

The idea of being "behind" only exists when life is treated like a race with a single timeline, a fixed order, and a shared finish line. But real lives don't unfold that way. They unfold through seasons, constraints, responsibilities, awakenings, and interruptions. You did not waste time—you gathered context. You did not delay—you carried weight. You did not fail to begin—you survived what you needed to survive before you could.

What you lived before you started was not a detour. It was preparation in disguise.

This is difficult to accept because comparison is so efficient. You can always find someone younger, faster, louder, more visible. Someone who seems to have started earlier and arrived sooner. But comparison strips context. It ignores what you carried, what you learned, what you endured. It reduces a life to a highlight reel and then asks you to measure yourself against it. That comparison was never fair—and it was never accurate.

Being "behind" assumes there was a correct sequence you failed to follow. But growth does not follow scripts. Some people start early and grow shallow. Others start late and grow deep. Some begin with confidence and collapse at the first obstacle. Others arrive hesitant and endure. Timing does not determine legitimacy. Engagement does.

What matters is not *when* you started, but *how honestly* you did.

This chapter exists to dismantle the shame of delayed beginnings. Shame tells you that your past disqualifies you. That the years you spent waiting, working, caregiving, surviving, doubting somehow invalidate your right to begin now. Shame is wrong. Those years didn't make you late—they made you ready in a way you couldn't have been before.

You see this clearly when you look at your capacity now. You handle discomfort differently. You tolerate uncertainty more skillfully. You ask better questions. You understand tradeoffs. You recognize patterns. These are not the traits of someone behind. They are the traits of someone seasoned.

Starting later often brings a different kind of courage. Not the reckless courage of someone with nothing to lose, but the grounded courage of someone who knows exactly what's at stake—and chooses movement anyway. That courage is quieter, but it's sturdier. It doesn't rely on adrenaline. It relies on resolve.

There is also a compassion that tends to emerge in those who start after waiting. You understand hesitation in others. You don't judge uncertainty as weakness. You know what it costs to begin. That compassion shapes how you lead, create, and relate. It makes your starting less about ego and more about meaning.

The belief that you're behind also misunderstands how life works. Life does not reward speed—it rewards alignment. Moving fast in the wrong direction is not progress. Waiting until you're able to move with integrity is not delay—it's discernment, even if you didn't name it that way at the time.

This chapter matters because if you believe you're behind, you'll always rush. You'll skip steps. You'll chase outcomes to prove worth. You'll build from urgency instead of intention.

Letting go of the "behind" narrative allows you to move at a pace that is sustainable, honest, and yours.

You are not late to your life.

You arrived exactly when you did because this is when you were capable of choosing consciously instead of reacting unconsciously. This is when you were able to start without abandoning yourself. This is when starting became an act of alignment rather than escape.

The past does not disqualify you.

It contextualizes you.

And once you stop telling yourself you're behind, something profound happens. The pressure lifts. The panic softens. You no longer feel the need to catch up to anyone. You are free to build deliberately, deeply, and in a way that reflects who you actually are.

You didn't miss your moment.

You became someone who could finally recognize it.

Chapter 34

The Only Question That Matters From Here

After everything you've explored—fear, waiting, identity, resistance, momentum, permission, confidence—there comes a moment where the noise quiets. Not because life suddenly becomes simple, but because the questions that once consumed you lose their urgency. You stop cycling through endless internal debates. You stop revisiting the same mental crossroads. What remains is one question—not loud, not dramatic, but steady and unavoidable.

Am I willing to keep choosing this?

Not forever.

Not perfectly.

Not without doubt.

Just this.

For a long time, your questions were abstract. *What should I do with my life? What's my purpose? What's the right path?* These questions feel important, but they're also paralyzing because they demand certainty before experience. They keep you oriented toward answers instead of action. The only question that actually moves a life forward is much smaller—and much harder to avoid.

Am I willing to continue?

This question strips away fantasy. It doesn't ask you to predict outcomes or justify decisions. It doesn't ask whether this will succeed, impress, or make sense to anyone else. It asks something more grounded: given what you now know, given how this feels, given who you are becoming—are you willing to take the next step?

This question matters because it honors reality. It acknowledges that clarity is partial, confidence fluctuates, and conditions are rarely ideal. It doesn't demand belief. It asks for consent. Consent to keep participating in your own life instead of postponing it.

There is relief in this question. You are no longer trying to solve your life all at once. You are no longer measuring yourself against imagined futures. You are simply deciding whether today's direction is honest enough to continue walking. That decision is lighter than certainty—but it is stronger.

The question also respects your agency. It does not trap you. You are not committing to a destination—you are committing to presence. If the answer changes later, you will answer again. That is not failure. That is responsiveness. The only thing this question does not allow is autopilot.

You may notice that when you ask this question sincerely, fear has less leverage. Fear thrives on distant outcomes and irreversible consequences. This question stays close. It keeps the decision human-sized. You are not choosing your entire future—you are choosing the next expression of integrity.

This is where many people finally stop over-intellectualizing their lives. They stop asking what they *should* want and start noticing what they are willing to sustain. Willingness becomes the compass. If you are willing to show up, to adjust, to learn, to remain in relationship with what you're building—that is enough to continue. If you're not, that information matters too. Either way, you are no longer avoiding the truth.

This chapter matters because it marks a transition from seeking answers to practicing authorship. You are no longer asking for permission from ideas, frameworks, or even this book. You are listening inward, not for certainty, but for resonance. For honesty. For the quiet yes or no that emerges when you stop negotiating and start acknowledging what's real.

The only question that matters from here is not about success, speed, or validation.

It's this: *Am I willing to choose this again tomorrow?*

If the answer is yes—even softly, even cautiously—that is starting.

If the answer is no—that is clarity, not defeat.

Either way, you are no longer waiting. You are responding.

And a life built from response rather than avoidance is a life that stays alive.

From here on, you don't need better answers.

You only need to keep answering honestly.

Chapter 35

Starting, Again

If this book has done its work, you may feel something unexpected at this point—not a rush of certainty, not a dramatic surge of motivation, but a quiet steadiness. A sense that nothing mystical is required from here. No transformation montage. No new identity announcement. Just a familiar, grounded truth settling into place:

You know how to start now.

Not in theory. In practice.

And that matters, because life will keep asking.

It will ask when things fall apart again.

It will ask when the work loses its shine.

It will ask when fear finds a new costume.

It will ask when success introduces unfamiliar pressure.

It will ask when you outgrow what once fit.

Starting was never a chapter you pass through and leave behind. It is the movement you return to when certainty fades. It is the skill that keeps you from freezing when the terrain changes. It is the difference between someone who waits for permission and someone who stays in relationship with their life.

This final chapter is not a conclusion. It's a reminder.

You will hesitate again.

You will doubt again.

You will feel the pull of comfort, approval, and certainty again. That doesn't mean anything went wrong. It means you're still alive.

What's different now is that hesitation no longer confuses you. You don't mistake it for a verdict. You don't ask it to leave before you move. You recognize it as a familiar companion at the edge of growth. You nod to it—and you take the step anyway.

Starting again doesn't require courage in the way you once imagined. It requires honesty. Honesty about where you are. Honesty about what matters. Honesty about the cost of staying still. That honesty is enough to move you forward, even when confidence hasn't caught up yet.

There will be moments when you forget all of this. When old patterns resurface. When waiting feels tempting again. That's not failure. That's the practice calling you back. Starting again is not a reset—it's a continuation. You don't lose what you've built because you pause. You lose it only if you abandon yourself entirely.

The most meaningful lives are not built by people who never stop. They are built by people who know how to return. Who don't dramatize the restart. Who don't shame themselves for needing it. Who simply begin again with what they know now.

You don't need this book anymore after this point. Not because it failed—but because it did its job. The ideas only mattered insofar as they led you back to yourself. Back to your agency. Back to your willingness to participate without guarantees.

Starting again might look small. It might look unimpressive. It might look nothing like what you once imagined.

That's fine.

The power was never in how it looked. It was always in the fact that you moved.

If there is one thing to carry forward, let it be this:

You don't wait for your life to make sense before you live it. You live it—and meaning reveals itself in motion.

Starting, again, is not a step backward. It is the most honest way forward.

And whenever you forget, whenever the noise returns, whenever the question resurfaces—you already know the answer. **You start.**

Chapter 36

The Power Was Never the Start

It's tempting to believe that the power lived in the moment you finally began. That everything changed because you crossed a line, made a decision, took a step. And while starting mattered—deeply—it was never the source of the power. Starting was simply the doorway. What changed your life was what came *after*: the relationship you built with yourself once you realized you could move without permission, clarity, or certainty.

The real power was not the act of starting. It was the realization that you are someone who can begin.

That distinction matters, because starting is an event, but becoming is a posture. Events happen once. Postures shape a life.

Before, you were oriented toward safety, approval, and readiness. You waited for conditions to align before you trusted yourself to move. After starting—and returning, and starting again—your orientation shifted. You learned that movement does not require resolution. That uncertainty is not a flaw in the process. That fear does not disappear, but it no longer defines the boundaries of your choices. The power was never the step. It was the *repatterning* that followed it.

You no longer see yourself as someone waiting for a green light. You see yourself as someone who navigates intersections. You assess. You choose. You proceed. Sometimes slowly. Sometimes imperfectly. But deliberately. This changes how you experience everything—work, relationships, creativity, aging, loss, opportunity. Life stops being something you prepare for and starts being something you engage with.

What's most important to understand is that this power does not make you invincible. It makes you resilient. You still feel disappointment. You still encounter setbacks. You still face moments where the path dissolves in front of you. The difference is that those moments no longer erase your sense of agency. You don't collapse into waiting. You orient, adjust, and begin again. That is real power.

This power is quiet. It doesn't demand recognition. It doesn't require confidence. It doesn't announce itself. In fact, from the outside, your life may not look radically different at all. The difference is internal—and internal differences compound. You spend less energy negotiating with fear. Less energy explaining yourself. Less energy rehearsing futures that never arrive. That energy gets reinvested into presence, learning, and participation.

You may notice that you are more patient now, but less tolerant of misalignment. More compassionate, but less willing to abandon yourself. More flexible, but less available for lives that require you to shrink. These are not contradictions. They are the natural outcomes of someone who trusts their ability to move through uncertainty rather than avoid it.

This chapter exists to clarify something essential: **the power of starting was never about change—it was about authorship.** You reclaimed the ability to participate in shaping your life instead of postponing it. You stopped asking life to guarantee safety and started asking yourself to stay honest. That shift does not end. It matures.

There will be new thresholds.

New fears with new vocabulary.

New reasons to wait that sound convincing.

When they come, you won't panic. You'll recognize the pattern. You'll remember that the power was never in eliminating hesitation—it was in not mistaking hesitation for a stop sign. You'll remember that clarity follows engagement. That identity follows behavior. That trust is built through response, not prediction.

If this book leaves you with anything, let it be this understanding:

You don't need to be ready to live a life that belongs to you. You need to be willing to stay in relationship with it.

The power was never the start. The power was becoming someone who no longer waits for their life to begin.

And that power—once reclaimed—is not something you lose.

It's something you live.

Chapter 37

This Is Where You Begin to Live It

There is a quiet moment after understanding settles, after insight lands, after the language finally matches something you've felt for a long time. It's the moment when you realize that nothing else needs to be added. No more frameworks. No more explanations. No more convincing. What remains is not an idea—it's a choice you're already making.

This chapter exists to mark that moment. Not as an ending, but as a handoff.

Up to now, starting may have felt like a concept you were learning to trust. Something you were practicing deliberately. Something you returned to when fear or hesitation resurfaced. But at some point, starting stops being something you *do* and becomes something you *live*. It fades into the background, not because it lost importance, but because it integrated.

You don't think, *I should start now.*

You think, *This is what I do next.*

That shift is subtle, but it changes everything.

Living it means you stop waiting for emotional alignment before acting. You stop needing the internal weather to be calm. You move through good days and bad days with the same basic posture: presence, response, continuation. The drama fades. The urgency softens. What remains is a steady engagement with your life as it is—not as you wish it were or fear it might become.

You will still encounter moments of pause. Decisions that carry weight. Transitions that feel tender. Living it does not make you immune to difficulty. It makes you capable within it. You no longer ask, *Can I handle this?* You ask, *How do I meet this honestly?* That question doesn't paralyze—it directs.

This is also where self-trust stops being something you think about and becomes something you rely on. You don't need to remind yourself that you're capable. You have evidence. You've watched yourself show up when it mattered. You've seen yourself adapt when things didn't go as planned. That trust doesn't shout—it supports.

Living it means your life becomes less performative. You're not trying to signal progress or justify your choices. You don't need every step to look impressive. You care more about coherence than applause. More about truth than speed. This doesn't make you smaller—it makes you grounded. And grounded people move far.

There is also a gentler relationship with ambition that forms here. Ambition no longer feels like pressure to become someone else. It feels like curiosity about who you can grow into. You don't chase goals to prove worth. You pursue direction because it feels alive. That difference changes how effort feels. It becomes expressive rather than compensatory.

This chapter matters because many people stop just short of integration. They understand the ideas. They feel inspired. But they continue to treat starting as something separate from life—something they must consciously summon. Integration is when the line dissolves. When life itself becomes the practice.

You won't always notice this happening. One day you'll simply realize that you handled something differently. That you didn't freeze. That you didn't wait for permission. That you didn't negotiate endlessly. You responded. You moved. You continued. And it felt... normal.

That's how you know it worked.

This is where the book steps back. Not because the journey is complete, but because it no longer needs narration. From here on, the work is lived in moments too small and too real to be captured on a page.

When fear returns, you won't need a reminder. When uncertainty appears, you won't need reassurance. When the next edge shows up, you won't need instruction.

You'll do what you've learned to do.

You'll start. You'll adjust. You'll continue.

Not because it's easy. Not because you're fearless. But because this is who you are now.

This is where the book ends. And this is where your life—fully participated in—continues.

Afterword

If you've reached this point, there's a good chance something in you has already shifted. Not in a way that's loud or obvious—but in a way that's difficult to undo. Once you see how waiting works, it's hard to pretend you don't. Once you recognize the patterns, they don't disappear—but they lose their authority.

This afterword is not here to summarize what you've read. You already know what the book was about. It was never really about starting a business, finding a partner, or chasing a dream. Those were only the surfaces. What this book explored—quietly, insistently—was your relationship with movement. With agency. With the moment you decide whether your life remains something you think about or something you participate in.

You may not feel transformed. That's okay. Transformation is often a story we tell *after* the fact. What matters is whether you feel more honest. More present. Less willing to hide behind good reasons. Less patient with postponement that pretends to be wisdom. Those shifts don't announce themselves—but they matter.

You will forget parts of this book.

You will remember sentences out of order.

You may come back to it years from now and read it differently.

That's how it's supposed to work.

What I hope stays with you is not a concept, but a posture. A way of meeting moments when hesitation shows up. A way of noticing when fear starts negotiating. A way of asking yourself—not dramatically, not endlessly—*what does starting look like here?*

You don't need to live boldly every day.

You don't need to be certain.

You don't need to have a plan that makes sense to anyone else.

You only need to remain available to your own life.

If this book has done its job, you'll recognize when you're waiting—not with shame, but with clarity. And when you recognize it, you'll know what to do next. Not because the book told you, but because you've learned how to respond.

There is no final arrival point. No version of you that never hesitates again. There is only a growing familiarity with beginnings. A quiet confidence in your ability to move without guarantees. A willingness to choose participation over postponement, again and again.

That is enough.

Wherever you go from here—slowly, imperfectly, quietly—I hope you keep choosing to stay in relationship with what matters to you. Not someday. Not when it's safe. But in the way that's possible now.

Thank you for reading.

More importantly—thank you for not waiting.

Acknowledgements

No book like this is written alone, even when most of it happens quietly.

I want to thank the people who didn't just support this book, but supported the *process* behind it—the uncertainty, the false starts, the long pauses, and the returning. The people who understood that this wasn't about writing words, but about telling the truth in a way that required patience and honesty.

To my family—thank you for being both my anchor and my mirror. For tolerating the times when I was physically present but mentally wrestling with ideas that refused to stay quiet. For reminding me, often without words, that life is not meant to be postponed in the name of responsibility alone.

To the mentors, partners, and colleagues I've worked alongside over the years—thank you for the conversations that challenged me, the disagreements that sharpened my thinking, and the real-world pressure that made theory irrelevant. This book was shaped as much by boardrooms, job sites, and difficult decisions as it was by reflection.

To the friends who asked nothing more than honesty—who didn't rush me, didn't try to fix me, and didn't need me to arrive fully formed—thank you. You created the space where starting felt possible without performance.

To those who trusted me before this book existed—clients, collaborators, and students—you reminded me that movement matters more than polish, and that clarity often shows up only after you step into the work.

And finally, to the reader.

Thank you for staying with this book until the end. Thank you for not skimming it for answers or rushing it for outcomes. If something here felt uncomfortably familiar, I hope you recognized that discomfort as recognition—not judgment. This book exists because people like you are willing to pause, reflect, and then continue.

If you start something because of this—quietly, imperfectly, without announcement—then every word was worth it.

— Manuel Rosendo

www.ingramcontent.com/pod-product-compliance
Lightning Source LLC
Chambersburg PA
CBHW020154090426
42734CB00008B/817